H. grollier.

A BOOK OF RUSSIAN VERSE

By C. M. Bowra

THE HERITAGE OF SYMBOLISM

A BOOK OF
RUSSIAN VERSE

*Translated into English by various hands
and edited by*

C. M. BOWRA

LONDON
MACMILLAN & CO. LTD
1943

PRINTED IN GREAT BRITAIN
BY R. & R. CLARK, LIMITED, EDINBURGH

PREFACE

THE aim of this book is to give a representative selection of short Russian poems in translations as faithful and as readable as can be found. In most cases, the versions follow not only the sense but the metres of the originals. The selection begins with Pushkin because with him Russian poetry really found itself, and it ends about 1922 because the poetry written after that date belongs to a different world and demands separate treatment. In compiling such a book it is a pleasure to record thanks both to authors and to publishers for permission to make use of poems already published, particularly to the Hon. Maurice Baring and Messrs. Heinemann for pieces from *Russian Lyrics*, to Mrs. Juliet Soskice and the Oxford University Press for extracts from *Who can be Happy and Free in Russia?*, to the Oxford University Press for poems by J. S. Phillimore in *Things New and Old*, to Professor Oliver Elton and the Liverpool University Press, the Pushkin Press and Edward Arnold respectively for selections from *A Sheaf of Papers*, *Evgeny Onegin* and *Verse from Pushkin*. To East and West Ltd. for a version from J. Pollen's *Russian Songs and Lyrics*, and to the *Slavonic Review* and its contributors, Professor R. M. Hewitt, Mrs. Maud F. Jerrold, Sir Bernard Pares, Dr. W. A. Morison, Mr. R. Christie, and Mr. W. Matthews for many valuable pieces. It was not my first intention to add many pieces of my own, but I seemed forced to do so by a desire to make the book really representative. I have no claims to be a Russian scholar, and I have persevered in my task simply because I have been helped and encouraged by generous friends, by Professor V. de S. Pinto who has both sent me poems of his own and made many useful suggestions, by Mr. John Betjeman who has aided me in the intricacies of English composition, and above all by Professor S. Konovalov who has lent me books otherwise unobtainable and devoted much of his valuable time to removing my grosser mistakes and helping me from his great knowledge. I hope that the kind services which these friends have rendered will help to give English readers at least some idea of the variety and richness of Russian poetry.

C. M. BOWRA

OXFORD, *June* 1943

CONTENTS

CONTENTS

CONTENTS

CONTENTS

xi

INTRODUCTION

RUSSIAN poetry is largely the creation of the nineteenth century and even of a single man. It is true that the heroic *Raid of Igor* was composed about 1185, that popular historical lays were known to English travellers in the reign of James I, that in the eighteenth century the language was reduced to order and even to verse by gifted pioneers. But Russian poetry, as we know it, owes an incalculable debt to Pushkin. In almost every kind of verse, in narrative, in drama, in fairy-tale, in ballad, in meditative lyric and in song, he created forms which his successors have used. He proved that Russian is a noble language for poetry and that it can be adapted to almost any kind of rhythm or metre. Above all he marked out a field and set limits to it which his successors abandoned at their peril. So great was his imaginative under-standing of his countrymen that he seems to have written about almost everything that matters in their lives, their hearts and their souls. Others have added to the range of his subjects or delved deeper into experiences on which he merely touched. Yet each departure from Pushkin's norm has usually been followed by a return to it, as if the adventure had been risky and it were safer to keep to the established bounds. It might almost be said that if we know Pushkin, we know the peculiar qualities of Russian poetry. Certainly in no other country does poetry owe so much to a single man.

When we come to Russian poetry from English or French or Italian, we feel at first that its tones are quieter, its colours more subdued, its subjects less adventurous, its range more limited. It is not merely that Russia has had no Renaissance, no Reformation, no *Grand Siècle*, nor that the centuries in which it was severed from Western Europe deprived it of the historical development which created our own civilisation; it is that even in the nineteenth century the world revealed in Russian poetry is much quieter, much closer to common life, than we should expect in the age of Shelley and Hugo. Even when it embarks on boldly imaginative subjects and makes use of the stupend-ous mountains and wild rivers of the Caucasus or tells again the immemorial fancies of its folk-tales, it somehow reduces even these to order and imposes upon them its characteristic moderation. Though its two greatest exponents, Pushkin and

Lermontov, lived lives at least as romantic as Byron's and were both killed in duels, their poetry is more straightforward and more truthful than his. Exaggeration, rhetoric, unfettered fancy, histrionic gestures, are not in the Russian tradition. However the poets behaved in their lives, in their work all is order and sincerity. In this Pushkin set a unique example. He combines the best qualities of the eighteenth century with the best of the Romantic Revival. His art has the assurance, the ease, the neatness, the finish of the Age of Reason without its pomposity, its pretentiousness, its exaggeration. His subjects have the emotional force, the imaginative vigour, the profoundly human appeal of the great Romantics without their flights into the inane. The most frankly emotional of European peoples has given to the arts the discipline which it sometimes shuns in its life. Its emotions are naturally so strong that it feels no call to exaggerate them or to dress them up in the hope of making them more interesting. It prefers the quiet phrase, the understatement, the precise, significant word. The result is that Russian poets, like Greek, succeed by never saying too much, by leaving the reader to supply half the effect and making him return to them in the confidence that at each reading of a poem he will always find something new in it.

This poetry is written in a language which deserves all that Turgenev said of it : " In days of doubt, in days of dreary musings on my country's fate, thou alone art my stay and support, mighty, true, free Russian speech ! But for thee, how not fall into despair, seeing all that is done at home ? But who can think that such a tongue is not the gift of a free people ? "[1] For poetry Russian is superbly fitted. Its rich and expressive syntax enables it to dispense with many artifices required by English. Its strong stress-accent allows it to fall easily into almost any kind of metre. Its varied and uncorrupted vowels, its abundance of liquid consonants, its combination of short and long words, its large vocabulary, its affectionate diminutives, all fit it for verse. It is rich in rhymes not merely single but double and even triple. It can have the monumental conciseness of Latin, the magnificence of English, the subtlety of French. The only language with which it may be compared is Greek, and to that it is inferior. For Greek has all the ease and fluency of Russian, all its adaptability and variety and expressiveness, but it is more muscular,

[1] Trans. Constance Garnett.

more masculine. It rises without effort to stern altitudes for which Russian is less well fitted. But with this exception, Russian is perhaps of all European languages the most gifted by nature for poetry. Its good fortune has been that though this poetry came late, it came under peculiarly good auspices and with the blessing of genius on it. The opportunity then offered to it has been amply taken.

Russian poetry is penetrated by the Russian landscape, with its vast spaces, its rolling steppes, its woods of pine and birch and fir. It is a country of long, bleak, snowbound winters, and of sudden, intoxicating springs, of great rivers and vast uninhabited distances. Its characteristic birds are the swan, the hawk and the crane, but in the spring and summer it abounds with nightingales which play their own part in its poetry from the classical allusiveness of Pushkin to the simple folk-songs of Koltsov. On the grassy steppes herds of horses wander at liberty ; when the harvest comes, the whole horizon encloses a single field. In this huge landscape the dwellings seem almost insignificant, and only occasionally do the poets mention them, as Alexey Tolstoy conveys the pathos of a decaying manor-house or Pushkin the poverty of his old nurse's hut. What really matter are the countryside, the changes of its seasons, its familiar and unchanging features. In its latest phase Russian poetry is still as attached to the country as it was in its beginnings, but it has never formed a metaphysical conception of nature like Wordsworth's or Shelley's. It is content to see and to enjoy nature as it is, as something apart from man and even from God. Nor is it the unusual in nature that normally attracts Russian poets. They are interested in its most ordinary manifestations, the coming of spring, the presence of clouds in the sky, the sudden onrush of storms, the breaking of the ice, the effects of snow. Even the mystical Tyutchev sings of spring in the most natural and direct way ; even so detached an artist as Fet confines himself to scenes which belong to almost any part of the Russian landscape ; Pushkin's account of a winter morning is the familiar experience of everyone. The Russian poets love nature with a simple and intense love which asks no support from metaphysics.

The simplicity of the landscape presents a contrast to the variety of human life in it and to the strange depths of human nature to be found in any man or woman. The Russian poets, like the Russian novelists, have a lively understanding of many kinds of humanity, and even in the short space of lyrical poetry they are able to present types so varied as the love-lorn peasants of Koltsov, the blind preacher of Polonsky, the soldiers of Lermontov, the young girls of Pushkin, the bricklayer of Kazin. But in all these what counts is not the external circumstance but the soul, not the variety of livelihood but the fundamental, unchanging nature behind it. In *Tatyana's Letter* Pushkin presents the particular feelings of a girl in a particular situation, but his poem is typical of almost all girls who know the agony and the desperation of first love. In *The Unreaped Field* Nekrasov makes a moving poem not merely from the pathos of a dead peasant whose work is left undone but from the whole hard struggle which poverty-stricken labourers must endure to win a livelihood. Such poems are not mere dramatic idylls. Of course they help to illustrate the Russian scene, but their special interest is their insight into human destinies and their universal significance.

In lyrical poetry this profound interest in human life is most often turned to the poet's own experience, and it is when Russian poets write about themselves that they win their greatest triumphs. In this intimate poetry the quiet art of understatement makes every word ring true and seem important. No poetry is at once so simple, so tender and so powerful as that in which Pushkin unlocks his heart. Short poems like *I loved you* and *To* —— contain situations which might be elaborated on a great scale, but much of their beauty lies in their concentration, their distilled power. This poetry lacks both rhetoric and irony. It is singularly direct and comes straight from the heart, whatever its mood may be, to pass into pure music in such a song as A. Tolstoy's *It was an early day of spring*, or into troubled melancholy in Lermontov's *The Cup of Life*, or into complex brooding in A. Akhmatova's *No, no, I did not love you*. It may suddenly break into new worlds of poetry as in Pushkin's *The Beauty* and be so sure of its success that we wonder why such a poem has never been written before. It can, at moments, touch on wilder and stranger themes, on dark apprehensions and wild ambitions and cosmic gloom. The doubts which Pushkin felt about man's place in the universe have been extended and deepened by Blok; the homesickness of exile, to which Lermontov gave so poignant expression, has in our own time taken many new and poignant forms. The emotional range of Russian poetry covers almost all the places of the heart, from the ecstatic joy of first love to mature affection and brooding memory and defeated despair. It embraces the simplest pleasure in natural beauty and the tortured doubts of men who feel that they have lost their place in the world. In it there is often an extraordinary tenderness, a warmth and generosity of feeling, a love which is self-effacing and self-sacrificing. Even when it turns to anger and bitterness, this poetry seems still to be based on singularly pure and tender affections. Its simple words come direct from the heart, and the first and greatest claim of Russian poetry lies in the candour and power with which it presents all the varied phases of the emotional life.

The claims of the heart, or of the flesh, are countered by the claims of the soul ; the sense of pleasure is haunted and corrected by a sense of sin. In *Remembrances* Pushkin struck a note which reverberates through Russian poetry, the note of guilt and remorse which may settle on a man and make him feel that his life is contemptible and worthless. In *The Steps of the Commander* Blok transposes the sense of guilt into a kind of supernatural vengeance. From such a feeling the poet turns to God, tries to abase himself before Him and to make peace with Him. So in his *Troparion* Tolstoy gives memorable words to the feeling that all flesh is dust and that its achievements are nothing. In the nineteenth century the Russians were as a whole hardly self-conscious about their religion. It was part of their inner life and of their social system. To it they turned for help in their struggles, for consolation in defeat, for self-abasement in glory or in death. It supplied a vast emotional need in them. Therefore they associated it with what was most positive and vital in themselves. For Pushkin it is an essential part of his creative life ; for Khomyakov it imparts dignity and meaning to labour ; for Blok it provides symbols to explain and exalt suffering. The devotional poetry of Russia keeps a close connection with ordinary life. It arises naturally from any intense situation. It does not move in a special, separate sphere but is remarkably simple and direct and makes little use of mythology or even of theology. In the Russian soul the love of God is a natural counterpart to the loves of men and exists side by side with them as a contrast, a corrective and a help.

This sense of another world may at times take special forms. In his magnificent poem *The Prophet* Pushkin suggests that the poet has a peculiar insight and knowledge which come from God, and other poets have drawn similar conclusions from the existence of poetical inspiration. It was but a small step from this to believing in a mystical conception of life, and from this few Russian poets are very far. There are signs of it in Tyutchev, but it found its fullest and boldest utterance in the Russian Symbolists. The proud claims which Balmont made in *I came into this world* are the natural development of a philosophy already formed by Solovyev and Sologub, that the only reality is that of the spirit and that the poet is specially gifted to understand it. This mysticism is not necessarily Christian, though the symbols of Christianity are often used by it. It is based on the belief that the world which the poet knows in his inspired moments is all that really matters and that his acquaintance with it frees him from many ordinary ties and responsibilities. That is why we find a kind of nihilism in Ivanov's *Beauty's Nomads* and in Gumilev's *I and You*, why Bryusov's *The Coming Huns* breathes so sinister a prophecy of destruction. For Blok this mystical experience became a central subject for poetry. In *Demon* and in *Artist* he shows both what the creative experience means for him and the catastrophic contrast which it presents to his other, prosaic life. This view of life may be made to embrace strange conclusions, but it too is part of the Russian heritage and comes naturally to a people which has for centuries had its saints and holy men. Even the Symbolists only carried to a logical conclusion what Pushkin had suggested.

In its main lines Russian poetry follows the lines which Pushkin marked out for it. Yet it has shown great capacity for growth and for variety, and it has changed with the times. Its development has not been regular. Russia cannot boast of an unbroken succession of poets. The first great wave of Pushkin and Lermontov, who adapted the subjects of Romanticism to classical expression, came to an end when Lermontov was killed in 1841 at the age of twenty-seven. For the greater part of the middle nineteenth century poetry was not popular and prose held first place in public esteem. But such poets as wrote and were in due course recognised, Maykov and Fet and Tolstoy, have rightly been called Parnassian. Their emotions are cooler, their art more detached, than that of the great age. Tolstoy has even a Tennysonian delicacy and sweetness. When these poets disappeared from the scene, poetry again faded from view until the revival of the 'nineties which lasted almost to the Revolution of 1917 and found its final expression in Blok. This movement began as an offshoot of French Symbolism, but soon became typically Russian and gave expression to characteristic qualities of the Russian nature. In its turn it yielded to something simpler and more direct in the work of Gumilev and Akhmatova and to those poets of ordinary life and lyrical feelings who now seem to hold the stage. In this irregular process Russian poetry has not only kept pace with European poetry in general but has given voice to the spiritual needs of different ages from its first Romantic longings to the detached aristocratic elegance of the middle nineteenth century and the advanced individualism of the early twentieth.

This poetry has been written against a varying political background, and has had to adapt itself to political control and censorship. No doubt these limited its range. In his later years Pushkin was kept under strict surveillance by Nicholas I, and his fretting spirit broke into such cries of complaint as *'Tis time, my friend, 'tis time*. The detached aestheticism of Tolstoy and Fet is a reflection of the age in which they lived. Art had to retire to the fastnesses of imagination. Yet the Russian poets, limited as no doubt they were in their choice of subjects, have always been remarkable for their compassion for the defeated and the doomed. From Pushkin's *Message to Siberia* to Blok's *Vulture* we hear a voice of consolation. Even the aristocratic Tolstoy wrote *The Convicts* about the hopeless yet unbroken spirit of prisoners, and much of the work of Nekrasov is touched with pity for the heart-breaking frustration in which the peasant lives. When the Revolution of 1917 reversed the roles, and the servants became the masters, such a poem as Mayakovsky's *Our March* breathes the boundless hopes of the triumphant proletariat. The Russian poets have on the whole kept their integrity and independence in politics. They have made use of such comment as has been allowed to them, and they have felt the tragedy and grandeur of their country's destiny.

It might even be said that this love of their country is, more than anything else, their most abiding characteristic. They are concerned not merely with the landscape and its inhabitants, but with its destiny. The note which Lermontov struck with such affection in *My Country* was but one of many. The Russian poets love an ideal Russia, a country which has a soul as well as a face, and can be the object of contempt and disgust as well as of devotion and admiration. When Blok quarrels with his country, he does not love her any the less. He simply contrasts the Russia of political ambitions with the ideal Russia of his dreams. Even in the angry passions of the Revolution Anna Akhmatova has kept her independence and written poems in which she has no illusions about her country's brutality and squalor but still believes in its divine destiny and sees it illumined with an unearthly light. Though Russian poetry owes something to impulses and examples from abroad, and at times turns to themes from remote times or places and gives a new meaning to them, in the end it comes back to its own country and draws strength again from that illimitable landscape and that passionate soul.

ALEXANDER PUSHKIN
(1799–1837)

The Prophet

WITH fainting soul athirst for Grace,
I wandered in a desert place,
And at the crossing of the ways
I saw a sixfold Seraph blaze;
He touched mine eyes with fingers light
As sleep that cometh in the night:
And like a frighted eagle's eyes,
They opened wide with prophecies.
He touched mine ears, and they were drowned
With tumult and a roaring sound:
I heard convulsion in the sky,
And flight of angel hosts on high,
And beasts that move beneath the sea,
And the sap creeping in the tree.
And bending to my mouth he wrung
From out of it my sinful tongue,
And all its lies and idle rust,
And 'twixt my lips a-perishing
A subtle serpent's forkèd sting
With right hand wet with blood he thrust.
And with his sword my breast he cleft,
My quaking heart thereout he reft,
And in the yawning of my breast
A coal of living fire he pressed.
Then in the desert I lay dead,
And God called unto me and said:
" Arise, and let My voice be heard,
Charged with My will go forth and span
The land and sea, and let My word
Lay waste with fire the heart of man."

(Hon. M. Baring)

Girls' Song

MAIDENS, O you pretty things,
Company of loving ones,
Maidens, go ye frolicking,
Darlings in your revelry !
Strike ye up your roundelay,
Roundelay and ritual ;
See ye lure the lad to us
Where we circle round about !

When we lure the lad to us,
When we see him distantly,
Darlings, let us scatter then
And with cherries pelt at him,
Cherries and with raspberries,
And with currants, ruddy ones !
Never come to listen at
Roundelays of ritual,
Never come to spy upon
This our maiden merriment !

(O. ELTON)

FRONTING amazed Cythera grows
A wondrous ever-blooming rose
Sacred to Venus, dearer far
Than all her votive blossoms are.
The north wind blows when Autumn closes
    And Paphos is in ruin laid,
But in a world of fading roses
    There grows one rose that will not fade.

(R. M. HEWITT)

O VIRGIN-ROSE, no blushes
    Confuse me for your chains.
Within the laurel-bushes
    The nightingale remains.

He, king but captive willing,
     Lives near the proud fair rose,
And through the darkness thrilling
     His tender music goes.

                    (Maud F. Jerrold)

Devils

Storm-clouds whirl and storm-clouds scurry;
From behind them pale moonlight
Flickers where the snowflakes hurry.
Dark the sky, and dark the night.
On and on the sleigh still bears me;
Ding-ding-ding the small bell's sound.
Though I would not, something scares me
In the unknown plains around.

" Go on, driver ! " . . . " I can't go, sir.
Horses find it hard to pull,
And my eyes are blind with snow, sir;
Drifts have blocked the whole road full.
Strike me, but I search it vainly !
We are lost ! What's to be done ?
'Tis a devil leads us, plainly,—
From the road would have us gone.

" Over there — Look ! See him playing,
Blowing, spitting in my eye.
In the ditch he sends a-straying
This poor horse, and makes him shy.
Like a milestone weird he glimmered;
There in front he stood upright;
Like a tiny spark he shimmered,
Vanished in the empty night."

Storm-clouds whirl and storm-clouds scurry;
From behind them pale moonlight
Flickers where the snowflakes hurry.
Dark the sky, and dark the night.

Tired, we have no strength for wheeling.
Bell stops jingling, suddenly.
Halt. . . . " What is the plain concealing ?
Who can tell you ? Wolf or tree ? "

Blizzard angry, blizzard crying,
Horses start and snort in fear.
Farther on again he's flying ;
In the night his eyes burn clear.
Horses now go forward, straining ;
Ding-ding-ding, the small bell's sound.
There I see the phantoms gaining
In the plain that whitens round.

Fiends past number, formless, curling
In the play of dim moonlight —
Demons manifold are whirling,
Like November leaves in flight !
Crowds of them ! Where do they hurry ?
Why this song in mournful pitch ?
Is it Brownie that they bury ?
Make they marriage for a witch ?

Storm-clouds whirl and storm-clouds scurry ;
From behind them pale moonlight
Flickers where the snowflakes hurry.
Dark the sky, and dark the night.
Onward run the devils, sailing
In the measureless inane,
And their howls and mournful wailing
Nearly tear my heart in twain.

(C. M. Bowra)

Winter Evening

(To his old Nurse)

In black skies a storm is streaming,
Snowy whirlwind, rude and wild,
Like a savage beast now screaming,
Now lamenting like a child,

4

On the roof dilapidated
Shakes the thatch with sudden shocks,
Like a traveller belated
Loudly on the window knocks.

Our poor hut is old and crazy,
Melancholy and unlit.
Why, old friend, so still and lazy,
By the window do you sit ?
Is there nothing you remember ?
Has the loud wind struck you dumb ?
Are you dropping off to slumber
With the spindle's drowsy hum ?

Let us drink, my friend, unshrinking
Helper in young manhood's pain.
Where's the cup ? Grief calls for drinking !
Hearts will now be glad again !
Sing the Tomtit ever watching
Silently beyond the sea,
Sing the Maiden who went fetching
Water, — in the dawn went she.

In black skies a storm is streaming,
Snowy whirlwind, rude and wild,
Like a savage beast now screaming,
Now lamenting like a child.
Let us drink, my friend, unshrinking
Helper in young manhood's pain.
Where's the cup ? Grief calls for drinking !
Hearts will now be glad again !

(C. M. BOWRA)

Winter Morning

MIRACULOUS morning ! Frost and sun !
But you, delightful friend, sleep on.
'Tis time for beauty to bestir.
Open your soft and drowsy eyes
To greet the Dawn in northern skies,
A northern star to welcome her.

Last night, remember, a wind blew ;
In the rough sky a thick mist grew,
And the moon, like a pallid smear,
Was yellow through the gloomy cloud.
In melancholy you sat bowed.
But now, look through the window there !

Snow underneath the clear blue skies
Glitters in sunlight as it lies ;
A gorgeous coverlet it glows.
Black though the wood's transparent screen,
The fir-trees through the frost are green ;
The streams are bright beneath the floes.

Now every room with amber light
Is blazing. Crackling with delight
The stove bursts into heat and flares.
It's good to sit and dream to-day ;
But won't you tell them get the sleigh
And harness up the chestnut mares ?

Across the slippery morning snow,
My sweet companion, we shall go
And let the restless horses race ;
We'll visit lonely fields of grass,
Woods where in summer none can pass,
And river-bank, my most loved place.

(C. M. Bowra)

Night Piece

I can't sleep, and there's no light,
    Mirk all round and restless slumber,
    Tickings near me without number,
Monotonous clock measuring night !

O you Fates with old wives' chatter,
    Sleepy night so softly swaying,
Life with mouselike pitter-patter,
    Why vex me, what are you saying ?

Boring whispers what implying ?
   Do you murmur or complain ?
Can't you tell me what you're seeking,
   Calling me or prophesying ?
Oh for someone to explain
   That dark language you are speaking !

                 (V. DE S. PINTO)

OVER the Georgian hills the night her mantle throws ;
   Softly the river sings to me,
And gently too my sorrow wraps me, but it glows
   Always, for it is full of thee.
Of thee, only of thee. . . . O my sorrow's a veil
   That guards me from the world's loud voice,
While my heart loves and burns anew : how can it fail
   To love and burn ? It has no choice.

                 (V. DE S. PINTO)

Tatyana's Letter

THAT I am writing you this letter
Will tell you all ; and you are free
Now to despise me ; and how better,
I wonder, could you punish me ?
But you, if you are sparing ever
One drop of pity for my fate,
Will not have left me desolate.

I wished at first, believe me, never
To say a word, and then my shame
Had been unknown to you ; small blame
Could I have hoped, but once a week
Here in our village, when you came,
To see you, and to hear you speak,
And pass a single word of greeting,
Think of you only, night and day,
And wait — until another meeting.
You are not sociable, they say ;
The solitude, the country bore you.
We are not smart in any way ;
But always had a welcome for you.

7

Why came you ? why to *us* ? alone,
In this forgotten hamlet hidden,
I never should have known you, known
This bitterness of pangs unbidden.
And these emotions would have slept,
My soul its quiet ignorance kept :
— So, in due season, might I find,
Who knows ? a husband to my mind ;
Have been a true wife — to another,
A pious honourable mother.

"Another !" . . . I would ne'er have given
To living man, this heart of mine !
This was the will of highest heaven,
This was appointed : — I am thine !
All my past life assurance gave
That we should meet — as though to bind me ;
God sent thee here, I know, to find me,
And thou wilt guard me to my grave. . . .

Thou camest oft in visions to me ;
Wert dear, although I knew not thee ;
Thy tones reverberated through me,
Thy gaze absorbed, enchanted me
Long since. . . . But no, I was not dreaming !
Straight, when thou camest, not in seeming,
I knew thee, I took fire, stood numb,
And my heart told me, " He is come ! "

Is it not so ? Of old believing
I heard thee speak, I listened there
To thee in quiet, giving care
To my poor folk, or while relieving
My sick and troubled soul in prayer.
Art thou, to-day, not he who came
Flashed through the luminous darkness, nearing
My very pillow ? just the same
Belovèd vision, reappearing ?

Art thou a guardian angel to me,
Or crafty tempter to undo me ?

8

Resolve my doubts and my confusion;
It may be, this is all for nought
And an untutored soul's illusion,
And fate quite otherwise has wrought.
But be it thus; henceforth I yield me,
And all my fate, into thy hand;
I weep, and here before thee stand,
Entreating only that thou shield me.

Conceive it : I am here, and lonely;
None understands me, and if only
My reason were not faint and weak!
But I am lost, unless I speak.
I wait on thee; one look will waken
The hopes with which my heart is shaken;
Or — the dream snap its heavy spell
At one reproach — deserved too well!

No more of this; I dread to read it;
Yet though I sink with fear and shame,
Your honour keeps me safe; I plead it,
And to it boldly put my name.

(O. ELTON)

Angel

At Eden's gateway, downward spying,
A gentle-hearted Angel shone;
A dark rebellious Demon flying
Passed over Hell's abyss and on.

The Spirit of doubt and of rejection
Beheld that Spirit clean and true;
And warmth unwilling of affection
Then first, uneasily, he knew.

" Farewell ! " he cried, " I saw thy vision.
Thou hast not shone on me in vain.
All heav'n I hold not in derision,
Nor all on earth do I disdain."

(C. M. BOWRA)

9

May 26, 1828

GIFT haphazard, unavailing,
Life, why wert thou given me ?
Why art thou to death unfailing
Sentenced by dark destiny ?

Who in harsh despotic fashion
Once from Nothing called me out,
Filled my soul with burning passion
Vexed and shook my mind with doubt ?

I can see no goal before me ;
Empty heart and idle mind.
Life monotonously o'er me
Roars, and leaves a wound behind.

(C. M. BOWRA)

Three Springs

O'ER the world's plain that stretches vastly, sadly,
Three hidden springs mysteriously flow ;
The fount of youth — a spring that surges madly,
Whose waters murmuring and sparkling go ;
Castalia's fount whose wave of inspiration
Sings where the exiles o'er the desert press ;
And last the fount that cools all heart's pulsation
With the cool waters of forgetfulness.

(MAUD F. JERROLD)

Remembrances

WHEN trade and traffic and all the noise of town
    Is dimmed, and on the streets and squares
The filmy curtain of the night sinks down
    With sleep, the recompense of cares,
To me the darkness brings nor sleep nor rest.
    A pageant of the torturing hours
Drags its slow course, and, writhing in my breast,
    A fangèd snake my heart devours.

My fears take form, and on the wearied brain
 Grief comes, in waves that overflow,
And Memory turns a scroll to tell again
 A legend that too well I know.
Reading the past with horror, shame, and dread,
 I tremble and I curse,
But the repentant tears, the bitter tears I shed
 Will not wash out a single verse.

(R. M. HEWITT)

A Prayer

HERMITS and blameless women full of Grace,
To raise the heart into celestial space,
In storm and strife below to strengthen it,
A host of holy orisons have writ;
But one of all the multitudinous host
Of orison and praise has moved me most,
A prayer repeated by the priest in Lent,
In the dark days of fasting and lament:
Upon my lips more often it will dwell —
And breathe on the faint soul a vital spell:
" O Ruler of my days ! Ward off from me
The evil angel of despondency
And sloth ; and let not from my lips be heard
The sharp repeating of the idle word ;
Save me from lust, that snake which lives within ;
And let me not be blind to my own sin,
Blind to my brother's trespass let me,
Quicken the spirit of consent in me,
Of love, long-suffering and of chastity."

(HON. M. BARING)

The Beauty

 ALL harmony, all marvel, she,
 Above the world and passionless :
 She rests serene shamefastedly
 In her triumphant loveliness ;

She looks around her left and right :
She has no rival and no peer :
The beauties of our pallid sphere
Have vanished in her blinding light.

Bound for whatever be your goal,
Though to a lover's tryst you speed,
However precious in your soul
A day-dream you may hide and feed ;
Yet, meeting her, unwillingly
You of a sudden dazed and mute
Shall halt devoutly to salute
Her beauty and her sanctity.

(Hon. M. Baring)

Day's rain is done. The rainy mist of night
Spreads on the sky, leaden apparel wearing,
And through the pine-trees, like a ghost appearing,
    The moon comes up with hidden light.
All in my soul drags me to dark surrender.
There, far away, rises the moon in splendour.
There all the air is drunk with evening heat,
There move the waters in a sumptuous sheet,
    And overhead the azure skies. . . .
It is the hour. From high hills she has gone
To sea-shores flooding in the waves' loud cries ;
    There, where the holy cliffs arise,
Now she sits melancholy and alone. . . .
Alone. . . . Before her none is weeping, fretting,
None, on his knees, is kissing her, forgetting ;
Alone. . . . To no one's lips is she betraying
Her shoulders, her wet lips, her snow-white bosom.

No one is worthy of her heavenly love.
'Tis true ? . . . Alone. . . . You weep. . . . I do not move.

Yet if . . .

(C. M. Bowra)

To ——

BOUND for your far-off native shore
From alien lands you went away ;
I shall remember evermore
The tears I shed upon that day.
My hands grew colder as they tried
To keep you from forsaking me ;
" End not," my soul to Heaven cried,
" The parting's dreadful agony ! "

But, you, whose lips with mine were blent
In bitterness, your lips tore free ;
From lands of sullen banishment
To other lands you summoned me.
You said to me : " When we shall meet,
Where skies of azure never end,
Within the olives' dark retreat,
That kiss shall come to life, my friend."

But there, alas ! where azure gleam
Irradiates the vaulted skies,
Beneath the cliff where waters dream,
You fell asleep no more to rise.
Your beauty in the grave's abyss,
Has vanished, and your misery —
Gone is the resurrection kiss. . . .
I wait for it.   It is for me.

(HON. M. BARING)

I'VE lived to bury my desires,
And see my dreams corrode with rust ;
Now all that's left are fruitless fires
That burn my empty heart to dust.

Struck by the storms of cruel Fate
My crown of summer bloom is sere ;
Alone and sad I watch and wait,
And wonder if the end is near.

As conquered by the last cold air,
When winter whistles in the wind,
Alone upon a branch that's bare
A trembling leaf is left behind.

(HON. M. BARING)

FOR the last time I risk caresses
In fancy on your darling face.
To waken dreams my strong heart presses,
And softly, shy of its distresses,
Your love for me it would retrace.

Our life is hurrying and changes ;
Everything changes ; we change too.
And him, whose song through passion ranges,
Gloom of the grave from you estranges ;
He, once your friend, is dead to you.

Take it, my friend far separated,
This last leave-taking of my heart,
As would a widow desolated,
Or friend from friend to exile fated,
In silent kiss before they part.

(C. M. BOWRA)

I THOUGHT my heart had lost the power
Of suffering love's gentle pain :
I said, " The past, the fleeting hour
Comes not again, comes not again.

" They've gone, the raptures and the longing,
The flattering dreams that shone so bright. . . ."
But as I spoke, they came back thronging,
Called up by Beauty's sovran might.

(V. DE S. PINTO)

14

I LOVED you once, and in my soul maybe
Love is not altogether dead to-day.
But you shall not be troubled more by me
I would not sadden you in any way.
I loved you silently and hopelessly,
Worn now with jealousy and now with shame ;
I loved so truly and so tenderly,—
God grant some other's love may be the same !

(C. M. BOWRA)

To A. P. Kern

I CALL to mind a moment's glory.
You stood before me, face to face,
Like to a vision transitory,
A spirit of immaculate grace.

In hopeless torments of surrender,
In worldly tumult and alarm,
Your voice long echoed low and tender,
My dreams were of your face's charm.

Years passed. Rude winds blew all asunder,
Scattered the dreams that once were mine,
And I forgot your voice so tender,
The features of your face divine.

To deserts and to darkness banished,
My days grew long with naught to do ;
My God, my inspiration vanished,
My tears, my life, my love for you.

My soul awakened and uprisen,
Again I see you face to face,
Like to a transitory vision,
A spirit of immaculate grace.

My heart beats fast in exultation,
And all for it begins anew,
With God again, and inspiration,
And life, and tears, and love for you.

(C. M. BOWRA)

Foreboding

ONCE again the storm-clouds hover
In the silence over me ;
Jealous Fate again hangs over,
Menacing my misery.
Shall I face my Fate, disdaining ?
Shall I bear it and display
All the patience uncomplaining
That was mine in youth's proud day ?

Tossed by stormy life and driven,
Careless of this storm I wait ;
Maybe I shall find a haven
To protect me from my Fate. . . .
But to part — my fear foretold it !
That dread hour we cannot flee.
Let me take your hand and hold it ;
For the last time give it me.

Kind and quiet Angel, hear me ;
Speak to me with soft good-byes.
You have been so mournful.   Near me
Let your sweet face fall or rise.
The remembrance of your caring
More than compensation pays
For the strength and pride and daring
And the hope of youthful days.

(C. M. BOWRA)

On the Death of Amalia Riznich

BENEATH blue skies of her own country, she
    Fell languishing and withering,
Faded at last ; and her young shade, maybe,
    Already touched me with its wing.
Between us is a line impassable.
    In vain I tried to wake my sense.
I heard indifferent lips of her death tell ;
    I listened with indifference.

So this is she I loved with soul afire,
    With spirit in so dolorous stress,
With such a sweet and languishing desire,
    Such suffering, such foolishness.
Where are love's torments ? In my heart, alack,
    For that poor shadow confident,
For sweet remembered days that come not back,
    I find no tear and no lament.

                (C. M. BOWRA)

THE heavy clouds at length are scattering.
O Star of sorrow, star of evening,
Thy ray has silvered the fast-fading plain,
The quiet gulf, the black rocks of the main.
I love thy feeble light in the far heaven,
It wakes old thoughts now unto slumber given.
Have I not seen thee rise, remembered Star,
Across the peaceful land where all things are
Dear to the heart ; where poplars stand in state
Along the vale, and myrtles delicate,
And gloomy cypresses, and evermore
The south winds sing. Along the hills and shore,
Full of sweet thoughts, in dreaming idleness,
In older days my feet were wont to press.

                (MAUD F. JERROLD)

The Cloud

LAST cloud of a storm that is scattered and over,
Alone in the skies of bright azure you hover,
Alone with sad shadows you float on your way,
Alone you throw gloom on the joy of the day.

By you all the heaven was lately confounded,
You were with the hideous lightning surrounded,
You rang the mysterious thunderclap out,
You rained on the earth that was thirsting in drought.

Enough, and begone! 'Tis no time for your power.
The earth is refreshed now, and finished the shower;
And the breeze that caresses the leaves as it flies
Will chase you away from the quieted skies.

(C. M. BOWRA)

The Poet

UNTIL the poet hears Apollo's
Call to the hallowed sacrifice,
The petty cares of life he follows,
And sunk in them his spirit lies.
His holy lyre remains unsounded;
His spirit sleeps in numbing rest,
By an unworthy world surrounded,
Himself perhaps unworthiest.

But once his ear, attentive, shakes
When the god-given word is stirring,
The poet's soul, its pinions whirring,
Is like an eagle that awakes.
Then wearied of all worldly playing,
He shuns the babble of the crowd;
The people's idol disobeying,
His haughty head remains unbowed.
He runs away, and wildly, proudly,
Comes full of riot, full of sound,
Where empty waters wash around
The shores and woods that echo loudly.

(C. M. BOWRA)

Message to Siberia

DEEP down in the Siberian mine,
Keep up your long-enduring pride;
Your mournful toil is not in vain,
Nor thoughts that rapturously ride.

Misfortune's sister, Hope, is true,
And in the subterranean night
Shall waken courage and delight.
The welcome day shall dawn for you.

18

Friendship and love shall gather round
And through the gloomy bars shall go ;
To you who labour to and fro
My liberating voice shall sound.

From you shall drop the heavy chain ;
The walls shall crumble, Liberty
At the gate greet you joyfully,
Brothers give you your swords again.

(C. M. Bowra)

Take not away my wits, O God !
Better the beggar's scrip and rod,
    To toil and not to eat !
It is not that I hold my mind
Of much account, or would not find
    The parting from it sweet.

If only they would set me free
To my own will, how glad I'd be
    To seek the forest's shade.
In fiery frenzies I would sing,
And in my dreams' tumultuous swing
    All thoughts of self would fade.

I'd listen to the water's noise
And, brimming full of careless joys,
    Gaze on the empty sky ;
Oh ! then I should be free and strong,
A wind to course the plains along
    Or make the forests fly.

The curse is, if you lose your sense,
They shun you like a pestilence,
    And all your ways are tied.
They'll chain you to a madman's yoke,
And through the prison-bars provoke
    You like a beast inside.

No more in darkness shall I hear
The nightingale's voice ringing clear
  Or the black woodland's strains,
But only comrades' shrieks of fright,
And keepers' curses in the night,
  And screams, and clank of chains.

(C. M. BOWRA)

Stanzas

WHEN down the loud streets I go straying,
To churches where the people stream,
Or sit where youth's wild thoughts are playing,
I yield myself up to my dream.

I say : " How fast the years are flowing !
How many of us vanish here !
To vaults eternal all are going ;
For some the time's already near."

I see a lonely oak-tree thriving,
And think : " This patriarch will stay,
My unremembered life surviving
As it survived my fathers' day."

I hold a child in my embraces,
And as I hold him, think : " Good-bye.
For you shall live in my old places ;
Days bloom for you, for me they die."

On every day, in every season,
My thoughts have kept Death near to me ;
As he advances, so my reason
Asks when his birthday is to be.

Where shall my fated end enfold me ?
In alien lands, at sea, in fight ?
Or shall some neighbour valley hold me
And clasp my frozen body tight ?

But though it matters not where lying
My senseless body shall decay,
Yet, near to my own threshold dying,
There above all I wish to stay.

Grant that beside the graveyard's portal
Young children play in life's delight,
And in her loveliness immortal
Uncaring Nature still shine bright !

(C. M. BOWRA)

'TIS time, my friend, 'tis time ! For rest the heart is aching ;
Days follow days in flight, and every day is taking
Fragments of being, while together you and I
Make plans to live. Look, all is dust, and we shall die.

No happiness, — but rest and freedom life possesses.
Long to an envied fate my dreaming fancy presses,
And long, a wearied servant, have I plotted flight
To some far cloister where are work and pure delight.

(C. M. BOWRA)

Elegy

As leaden as the aftermath of wine
Is the dead mirth of my delirious days ;
And as wine waxes strong with age, so weighs
More heavily the past on my decline.
My path is dim. The future's troubled sea
Foretokens only toil and grief to me.
But oh ! my friends, I do not ask to die !
I crave more life, more dreams, more agony !
Midmost the care, the panic, the distress,
I know that I shall taste of happiness.
Once more I shall be drunk on strains divine,
Be moved to tears by musings that are mine ;
And haply when the last sad hour draws nigh,
Love with a farewell smile may gild the sky.

(HON. M. BARING)

21

Monument

I'VE built my monument, but not with hands I made it ;
Where the crowds flock to it, no grass shall ever grow.
With an unruly head it soars, and in its shade it
Leaves Alexander's Pillar low.

Not all of me shall die ! My secret lyre shall show it
And make my soul outlive the dust and fly decay.
And I shall be renowned while lives a single poet
On earth beneath the eye of day.

Through all great Russia's spaces shall my name be spoken,
And every living tongue of man my name shall tell ;
Proud breed of Slav, and Finn, and Tungus still unbroken,
And Kalmuck whom the steppe knows well.

And I shall for long years be loved by all the nation
Because for noble passions with my lyre I call,
Because in pitiless days I prayed for liberation,
Asked clemency for those who fall.

Listen to God's commands, my Muse, not disobeying ;
Fear not rebuke nor ask to win the crown of bay,
Indifferent to praise and censure, nothing saying
To fools, but let them have their say.

(C. M. BOWRA)

EVGENI BARATYNSKY
(1800–1844)

Death

I CALL not Death the child of darkness,
Nor, with the fancy of a slave,
Give him a scythe to arm his starkness
Nor skeleton from out the grave.

O offspring of the air our master,
O ornament with brilliant charms,
You bear no scythe that brings disaster
But peaceful olive in your arms.

When first the world arose in flowers
From raging forces matched and blent,
To you a guardian's rule and powers
Were trusted by the Omnipotent.

And flying over all creation
To harmony you straighten strife,
And there with cooling exhalation
You tame the violence of life.

You overcome the mutinous riot
And mad strength of the hurricane ;
You turn the ocean back in quiet
To hasten to its shores again.

In plants you set the bounds to growing,
That no gigantic wood may rise
O'er earth with ruinous shadows blowing,
That grass may grow not to the skies.

And what of man ? O holy Maiden,
When you have come, all angry fire
Dies out with which his cheeks were laden,
Flies all lascivious desire.

To your impartial justice presses
The crowd when sickness is its fate ;
And that same hand of yours caresses
Both servitor and potentate.

Force and confusion are our being,
Conditions of our tangled day.
But, us from every riddle freeing,
From us all chains you cast away.

(C. M. Bowra)

FEDOR TYUTCHEV
(1803–1873)

Spring Thunder

I LIKE a storm at May's beginning,
  When Spring's first thunder with wild cries,
As though in frolic gaily spinning
  Rumbles all round the pale-blue skies.

Then the young thunderbolts are clanging,
  Rain splashes, up the dust is borne,
From dripping boughs bright pearls are hanging,
  The sunshine gilds the young green corn.

Swift torrents rush from their hill fountains,
  Woods from their depths bird-music pour ;
Jargon of forests, brawl of the mountains . . .
  All gaily echo the thunder's roar.

(V. DE S. PINTO)

DEAR one, I love thine eyes, amazed
  By their quick play and brilliancy ;
When of a sudden they are raised,
  It is as if the whole wide sky
With heavenly lightning burned and blazed.

But stronger magic doth inspire
  Those eyes when suddenly cast down
In fevered moments of desire ;
  And through the drooping lids 'tis shown
Passion has lit her smouldering fire.

(MAUD F. JERROLD)

SHE sat upon the ground ; there lay
  A heap of letters by her side ;
She tore and flung them all away,
  Ashes from which the fire had died.

Lines so familiar to her sight
   She looked at with estrangèd air :
Thus souls might gaze from some far height
   On bodies they were wont to bear.

How much of her was here that she
   Would irretrievably destroy !
What better moments ceased to be,
   What memories of love and joy !

Silent and sad I stood apart,
   And fain upon my knees to fall,
Feeling as though upon my heart
   Darkness descended like a pall.

(MAUD F. JERROLD)

VOUCHSAFE, O Lord, Thy consolation
To him who in the summer's heat
Must go in beggarly privation
Past gardens down the sultry street.

Across the wall his glances wander
To grassy floors and shady trees ;
But unapproachably asunder
The lawns in cool abundance please.

'Tis not for him, the friendly greeting
Of trees that spread their shadows there ;
'Tis not for him, the water fleeting
From fountains, like a cloud in air.

The grotto's call is unavailing
From where its azure mist is spread ;
The fountain's dewy foam unfailing
Will never cool his fevered head.

Vouchsafe, O Lord, Thy consolation
To him who on life's road in heat
Must go in beggarly privation
Past gardens down the sultry street.

(ANON.)

26

On the horizon rises holy Night,
And Day, who comforts us, Day, whom we love,
Withdraws her coverlet of golden light
That covered the abysses from above.

And vision-like the outer world has gone.
Man, like an orphan in his homelessness,
Stands naked, all his force and strength fordone,
Face to face over that obscure abyss.

A dream that long ago passed out of sight
Seems all that light and living brilliance,
And in the strange inexplicable night
He learns the fated legacy of chance.

(C. M. Bowra)

The night was dark with indignation,
With cloud the sky was shrouded deep;
It was not threat nor meditation,
But drugged uncomfortable sleep.

Only the lightning's summer revels
Flashed alternating, out and in,
As if a horde of deaf-mute devils
Were holding conference of sin.

As if a sign agreed were given,
Broad conflagrations fired the sky,
And momently from the dark heaven
Woods and far forests met the eye.

Then disappeared again the vision;
In visible darkness all was pent
As if some great and dire decision
Were taken in the firmament.

(Anon.)

WHY, O willow, to the river
Leans thy head low, and why
Dost thou with long leaves that tremble,
And that thirsting lips resemble
Catch the ripples dancing by ?
Though thy leaflets faint and quiver,
Mirrored in a fleeting stream,
Yet the current speeds and splashes,
In caressing sunshine flashes,
And but mocks thy empty dream.

(W. A. MORISON)

NAY, in a poet put no trust,
Nor call him thine, my little maid ;
Fear thou his anger, if thou must,
But of his love be more afraid.

Take him not to thee, nor unite
Consenting marriage of two souls ;
Let not thy virgin veil, so light,
Harbour this handful of live coals.

His wit runs like an element,
Yet o'er himself he has no sway ;
His wreath, tho' not by his intent,
Will eat the curls of youth away.

The idle multitude mistake
Who speak him fair, and then reproach :
He has no venom like the snake,
But like a bee, lays hearts abroach.

Fear not that with his hands the poet
Will tear the sanctuary shrouds ; —
He'll strangle thee before he know it,
And spirit thee beyond the clouds.

(After J. S. PHILLIMORE)

No sickness of the flesh is ours to-day
   Whose time is spent in grieving and despairing ;
Who pray all night that night will pass away —
   Who greet the dawn rebelliously, uncaring.

Withered and parched by unbelief, the soul
   Impossible, unbearable things is bearing.
We are lost men, and ruin is our goal,
   Athirst for faith, to beg for faith not daring.

                (R. Christie)

Silentium

Be no word spoken.   Hide away
Thought and feeling day by day.
Let them rise and pour their light
And set like planets in the night,
Unheralded, unpraised, unheard.
Watch them, love them, say no word.

Heart knows not to speak with heart.
Song and speech can ne'er impart
Faith by which we live and die ;
A thought once spoken is a lie.
Unbroken, undefiled, unstirred
Thy fountain : drink, and say no word.

Live within thyself, and be
In a world of faerie,
Of magic thoughts that hide away
From the noise and glare of day,
Delicate airs on earth unheard,
Mark them, love them, say no word.

              (R. M. Hewitt)

ALEXEY KHOMYAKOV
(1804–1860)

The Labourer

ALL day, so long as arms had power,
  Through clinging clods of weedy waste,
The heavy plough of patient plougher
  Full long enough its path has traced.

Enough ! with savage spite surrounded,
  While fools malign and scoffers flout,
I have toiled, as though with strength unbounded ;
  I am worn out.   I am worn out.

'Tis time to rest.   O waters purling
  And leafy trees, and plains that drowse,
And high above my dingle curling
  The arches of the twining boughs.

If only for one moment, bending
  Beside the stream in that dear nook,
To drain, my thirsty lungs extending,
  The evening fragrance of the brook !

To wipe my brow from noon-day swelter
  Till all the load of cares was gone !
" Thou foolish one !   For thee no shelter !
  For thee no rest !   Go on !   still on !

" Look at the field !   How much to claim thee !
  How few the hours that still remain !
Arise ! and let no weakness shame thee !
  Thy Master bids.   Set forth again !

" 'Twas at a precious price I bought thee !
  The Cross, the Life-blood were the pay ;
Bend, tiller, o'er the task I taught thee !
  Toil, toiler, all the livelong day ! "

Before Thy high commandment humbled,
  O Lord, I tremble and submit,
And that Thy foolish servant grumbled,
  Record not at Thy judgment-seat!

With toil and sweat still undiminished,
  I will complete what Thou dost ask.
I will not sleep till it is finished;
  I will not weaken at my task.

Thy lazy servant shall not tarry;
  Firm in his hands the plough shall be,
Until the field Thou bidst him harry
  Is ready to be sown by Thee.

(SIR BERNARD PARES)

ALEXEY KOLTSOV
(1808–1842)

Song

SING not, nightingale,
Under my window ;
Fly away to the woods
Of my own country !
Learn to love the window
Of my soul's maiden !
Sing to her tenderly
Of my agony ;
Sing of me without her,
Waning, withering,
As the grass on the steppe,
Autumn facing it.
Without her, at night,
The moon's overcast ;
At midday, without flame
The sun goes its way.
Without her, who will now
Give me kind greeting ?
And on whose breast shall I
Lay my head in repose ?
Without her, whose word shall
Win a smile from me ?
Whose song, whose welcoming
Shall now touch my heart ?
Why sing, nightingale,
Under my window ?
Fly away, fly away,
To my soul's maiden !

(C. M. BOWRA)

Do not rustle, rye,
In the ripened ear !
Mower, sing no song
Of the spreading steepe !

There's no cause for me
To make money now.
In my youth I saved
And put money by,
Not for my own sake
But for her I loved.
It was sweet for me
In her eyes to gaze,
Eyes that brimmed so full
With sweet loving thoughts.
But alas ! those eyes
That were bright, are dim ;
In the sleep of the grave
Sleeps my lovely girl.
Heavy like a hill,
And as midnight dark,
Thoughts have settled down
Black upon my heart.

(C. M. Bowra)

Old Man's Song

I SHALL saddle my horse,
And on my fast horse
I shall gallop and fly,
Than a hawk more light,
Across fields, over sea,
To lands far away.
I shall summon and find
My lost youth again.
I'll be strong, I'll be great
In the youth once mine.
And again I shall please
Lovely young maidens.
But alas ! is no road
To what's past recall.
Never, never shall rise
The sun out of the west !

(C. M. Bowra)

33

Woman's Song

WINDS are blowing,
Rough winds boisterous,
Clouds advancing,
Cloudy darknesses ;
And the bright world
Disappears wholly,
And the fair sun
Disappears wholly.
In the damp mist
Nought but vaporous
Night behind it
Comes on darkening.
In this season
Of foul weather
Living alone
Gives the heart a chill.
What he needs is
Another bosom,
A burning soul,
A fair maiden.
With her, winter
Is warm summer,
In bad fortune
Sorrow's no sorrow.

(ANON.)

The Nightingale

THE nightingale, the rose's lover,
Through night and day sings songs above her,
But silent in her dream of innocence
She hears the strain but catches not the sense.
So oft a poet, singing to his lyre,
Pours in a maiden's ear his heart's desire ;
His fiery passion throbs through every tone,
But to the gentle maid it rests unknown.
For whom, she asks, is meant this song of his,
And wherefore sings he songs as sad as this ?

(MAUD F. JERROLD)

A Hawk's Thoughts

SHALL I live always
Sitting at home?
Wasting my youth here,
Never to roam?

And by the window
Shall I always stay,
The far road watching
By night and by day?

Are the hawk's pinions
Unfettered never?
Is ev'ry journey
Barred him for ever?

To foreign peoples
Fears he to be gone?
With step-mother Fortune
To live alone?

Why is he eager
To see all the world?
Why yearns his spirit
For pinions unfurled?

Why does my darling.
Oh why does she,
Her tears fast flowing,
Sit always by me?

See, she flies from me,
Sings me a song,
With her hand beckons
To follow along!

No, here no longer
At home shall I stay,
Nor watch at the window
The road far away!

I shall go out of doors ;
The road calls to a land,
And there I shall live
As God may command !

(Anon.)

MIKHAIL LERMONTOV
(1814–1841)

My Country

PATRIOT I am, but in so strange a fashion
No reasons of the mind must rule this passion.
Russia's blood-purchased glory,
The calm that best her haughty trust beseems,
Her dark and ancient day of hallowed story :
— 'Tis none of these that prompts my happier dreams.

I love her steppe, — I know not why it is, —
Better, the steppe and the cold silences ;
Forests that wave illimitable and free ;
And river-floods big-brimming like a sea.
And oh ! a sleigh that posts
Along a byway track, — and unaware
You meet a tardy beam that pricks the proof
Shadow of night, — the spirit of hearth and roof
Far out upon the air !
The trembling fire some wretched hovel boasts !

Give me the smoke of stubblefields alight :
A caravan of nomad wains that winds
Across the enormous weald ;
And on the hill, in the dun fallowfield,
A pair of stems, two birches glistening white !
I take such joy as many men know not,
To see a barn-door heaped, a straw-thatched cot,
A window and the carven shutter-blinds.
Some dewy holiday evening I'll sit by
To watch them dance, long hours, nor tire — not I —
Of the trampling and the whistling : how it glads
The heart to hear their talk, these tipsy lads !

(J. S. PHILLIMORE)

Hope

I HAVE a bird of paradise ;
Upon a springing cypress-tree
She sits for hours while daylight flies,
And not a song by day sings she.
Her back is of celestial blue,
Her head is purple ; flaming dye
Upon her wings, of golden hue
Like dawn's reflection in the sky.
Only when earth is slumbering,
Hidden, as night mists silent roll,
Upon her bough she starts to sing
So sweetly, sweetly to the soul,
That forced by it, your load of pain
Forgetting, you must sing away,
And in your heart each tender strain
Is a dear friend who comes to stay.
Often in tempests I have heard
That song which means so much to me,
And always for my peaceful bird
I listen, listen hopefully.

(C. M. BOWRA)

The Crag

IN the night a golden cloudlet straying
    Slumbered on a crag's breast, huge and burly ;
    Rose the damsel in the morning early,
Gaily fled through heaven's azure, playing.

But upon the wrinkled rock remaining
    Faintly still a trace of brightness wandered :
    Lone the giant stood, and deeply pondered
Softly, for air's emptiness complaining.

(V. DE S. PINTO)

Prayer

WHEN life's oppressive hour is mine
And in my heart griefs crowd,
A prayer of wondrous power is mine
That I repeat aloud.

Blest is the strength that flows to me
In concords of sweet sound;
Past reckoning it blows to me
Divine enchantment round.

Doubt, like a burden, leaping then
Far from the spirit flies;
From words of faith and weeping then
How light, how light we rise!

(C. M. BOWRA)

The Cup of Life

WE drink the cup of life while yet
 A veil our eyes is keeping;
And the cup's golden brim is wet
 With tears of our own weeping.

But when the veil falls from our eyes,
 As Death appears before us,
Then with the veil the mystery flies
 That held enchantment o'er us.

Oh then we see the golden cup
 Was empty in its gleaming,
That only dreaming filled it up,
 Nor even ours the dreaming!

(C. M. BOWRA)

The Angel

AN Angel was flying through night's deep blue,
 And softly he sang as he flew.
Noon, stars and clouds in a wondering throng
 Listened rapt by that heavenly song.

He sang of the blest, who live without stain
 In God's garden, a shining train.
He hymned the Lord's might, and his voice rang clear,
 For he sang without guile or fear.

He bore in his arms a young soul to its birth
 On the dark and sinful earth,
And the Angel's song remained in the soul
 Without words yet unblemished and whole.

Long after on earth when the soul would tire,
 It felt a strange, aching desire
For the music of heaven which it sought for in vain
 In earth's songs of sorrow and pain.

(V. DE S. PINTO)

WHEN o'er the yellowing corn a fleeting shadow rushes,
And fragrant forest glades re-echo in the breeze,
And in the garden depths the ripe plum hides its blushes
Within the luscious shade of brightly verdant trees ;

When bathed in scented dew, the silver lily,
At golden morn or evening shot with red,
From out behind a leafy bush peeps shyly,
And nods with friendly mien its dainty head ;

When down the shady glen the bubbling streamlet dances,
And lulling thought to sleep with its incessant song,
Lips me the secrets, with a thousand glances,
Of that still corner where it speeds along ;

Then does my troubled soul find solace for a while,
Then vanish for a time the furrows from my brow,
And happiness is mine a moment here below,
    And in the skies I see God smile.

(W. A. Morison)

    We parted, but my heart still wears
        Thine image, gracious yet,
    Pale token of those better years
        I never can forget.

    What though new passions rule my will?
        Deserted and untrod
    The temple is a temple still,
        The idol still a god.

(Maud F. Jerrold)

Why

I'm sad for, loving thee, I know full well
That this world's talk, with its calumnious spell,
Will never spare thy fresh youth's opening flower.
For every happy day and sunny hour,
Fate will exact in grief and tears his pay.
I'm sad because I see my loved one gay!

(J. Pollen)

A Sail

    A solitary sail that rises
    White in the blue mist on the foam, —
    What is it in far lands it prizes?
    What does it leave behind at home?

    Whistles the wind, the waves are playing,
    The labouring masthead groans and creaks.
    Ah, not from pleasure is it straying,
    It is not pleasure that it seeks.

41

Beneath, the azure current floweth;
Above, the golden sunlight glows.
Rebellious, the storms it wooeth,
As if the storms could give repose.

(C. M. Bowra)

No, not for you, for you, does my love flame;
'Tis not for me, your beauty brightly shining.
In you my love is for old anguish pining,
For youth once mine before disaster came.

And when at times I look into your eyes
And dwell on them with long and lingering glances,
I converse in mysterious utterances, —
'Tis not in words to you that my heart lies.

I speak to a companion of young days;
In yours, I seek another's face once cherished,
In living lips, lips that have long since perished,
In eyes, a flame that was long since ablaze.

(C. M. Bowra)

Do you remember how together
We said good-bye in evening weather?
Loud was the cannon's curfew sound.
To it across the waves we listened.
The setting sun no longer glistened,
And on the sea mist gathered round.
The straining shock passed through the air,
And suddenly died everywhere.

When the day's work is done at last,
How often then I dream about you!
The empty sea I wander past
And hear the curfew-shot without you.
When its loud echo comes again
From the grey waters back to me,
I weep, worn out by sorrow's pain,
And long to perish in the sea!

(C. M. Bowra)

Lone, I wander where the pathway glistens
In the mist with twinkling points of spar ;
Night is still, to God the desert listens,
And in heaven star communes with star.

Solemn wonder holds the heights of heaven,
Earth in cold blue radiance sleeps, and yet
Why am I with pain and anguish riven ?
Why this expectation ? this regret ?

Nothing now in life tempts my desiring,
Nothing in the past claims my regret ;
Peace and freedom are all my requiring, —
Ah, could I sleep soundly and forget !

No, not in the grave's cold sleep to moulder, —
I would lie in everlasting rest,
So but in me living forces smoulder,
So but tranquil breathing stir my breast,

So but, night and daytime, those that love me
Lull my ear with songs to drowse and drowse,
And an oak-tree, ever green, above me
Stoop, and make a dusk of murmuring boughs.

(After J. S. Phillimore)

Oh gloomy and dreary ! and no one to stretch out a hand
  In hours when the soul nears disaster. . . .
Desire ! but what use is an empty desire without end ?
  And the years, the best years, but fly faster.

To love ! yes, but whom ? It is nothing in time's little space.
  No love has an endless to-morrow !
Just look at yourself : what is past does not leave any trace.
  They are nothing, — both pleasure and sorrow.

What is passion ? That sickness so sweet, either early or late,
  Will vanish at reason's protesting ;
And life, if you ever, attentive and cool, contemplate,
  Is but empty and meaningless jesting.

(C. M. Bowra)

Clouds

CLOUDS in the skies above, hastily scurrying
Over blue steppes, in a pearly row endlessly,
Are you, as I am, to banishment hurrying,
From the lov'd North to the South going friendlessly?

Who is compelling you? Destiny's ruthlessness?
Envy concealed? or discover'd iniquity?
Or is it friends with a venomous truthlessness?
Is it the burden of sinful obliquity?

No! you are weary of fields lying wastingly. . . .
Strangers to passion and strangers to punishment,
Always at liberty, cold everlastingly,
You have no country, you know not of banishment!

(ANON.)

The Testament

I WANT to be alone with you,
A moment quite alone.
The minutes left to me are few,
They say I'll soon be gone.
And you are going home on leave,
Then say . . . but why? I do believe
There's not a soul who'll greatly care
To hear about me over there.

And yet if someone questions you,
Whoever it may be, —
Tell them a bullet hit me through
The chest, — and did for me.
And say I died, and for the Tsar,
And say what fools the doctors are :—
And that I shook you by the hand,
And spoke about my native land.

My father and my mother, both,
By now are surely dead —
To tell the truth, I would be loth
To send them tears to shed.
If one of them is living, say
I'm bad at writing home, and they
Have told the regiment to pack, —
And that I shan't be coming back.

We had a neighbour, as you know,
And you remember I
And she. . . . How very long ago
It is we said good-bye !
She won't ask after me, nor care,
But tell her ev'rything, don't spare
Her empty heart ; and let her cry ; —
To her it doesn't signify.

(Hon. M. Baring)

Cossack Cradle-Song

Softly, pretty baby, sleeping,
  Bayushki-bayú,
Quiet moon bright watch is keeping
  On your crib for you.
I shall tell you tales past number,
  Sing you ditties too.
Close your tender eyes in slumber,
  Bayushki-bayú.

Terek on his stones is fretting
  With a troubled roar ;
Wild Chechén, his dagger whetting,
  Crawls along the shore.
But your father knows war's riot,
  Knows what he must do.
Sleep, my darling, sleep in quiet,
  Bayushki-bayú.

You will learn — the time is nearing —
 All a soldier's ways ;
Foot in stirrup, never fearing,
 Rifle you will raise.
Silk for battle I shall deftly
 On your saddle sew ;
Sleep, my own sweet child, sleep softly,
 Bayushkí-bayú.

You will show a fighter's mettle,
 Cossack to the heart ;
I shall see you ride to battle,
 Wave your hand and start.
All that night in secret weeping
 My sad tears shall flow.
Soft, my angel, sweetly sleeping,
 Bayushkí-bayú.

I shall find that life is dreary ;
 Comfortless I'll wait,
Daily pray till I am weary,
 Nightly guess your fate,
Dream of you in countries going
 That are naught to you.
Sleep, my darling, care not knowing,
 Bayushkí-bayú.

I shall give to you a holy
 Picture for your way.
Think of God with it, and lowly
 Kneel to Him and pray.
Keep, when for war's danger arming,
 My remembrance true.
Sleep, my little baby charming,
 Bayushkí-bayú.

(C. M. Bowra)

Circassian Song

In our hills the girls are plenty :
  Starry night is in their eyes.
Live with them — the choice may tempt ye :
  Freedom's still the better prize.
    Oh be not so rash, my lad !
      Harkee, do not wed !
    Better keep your cash, my lad,
      And buy a horse instead !

He that has the mind to marry
  Takes the worser part, say I.
Off to fight the Russ ? " No hurry ! "
  Why ? Because the wife will cry !
    Oh be not so rash, my lad !
      Harkee, do not wed !
    Better keep your cash, my lad,
      And buy a horse instead !

An honest horse, he never changes ;
  He will go through flood and flame ;
Like a wind the steppe he ranges ;
  Far and near with him's the same.
    Oh be not so rash, my lad !
      Harkee, do not wed !
    Better keep your cash, my lad,
      And buy a horse instead !

(J. S. Phillimore)

The Veteran's Grave

He sleeps in his last sleep, long time
  He sleeps in his last sleep :
Green breadths of grass approach and climb
  To roof his earthen heap.

Hoar ringlets of the patriarch moulder
  Mixt in the paste of clay ;
Time was, they wagged upon his shoulder
  And dipped in goblets gay —

Oh ringlets white as foam of seas
    Against the headland flung !
The cold has froze what nought could freeze,
    The sweet counsels of his tongue.

The dead man's cheeks, they're full as pale
    As his foes' faces grew
Pale, when their ranked array to assail
    Alone he rose to view.

Damp sods his breast do bury,
    But that's no burden now :
The worm, all undisturbed and merry,
    Pries in and out his brow.

Lived he for this ?   Drew sword for this ? —
    That, come the hour of dark,
The eagles of the wilderness
    Should perch on his green ark ?

Had he no bards — that name, that strife
    In the mind of men to keep ?
Why, song's but song, and life's but life —
    He sleeps in his last sleep.

                    (J. S. PHILLIMORE)

The Prophet

THE Eternal Justice made me seer,
    All secret things to penetrate :
Since when, through eyes of men I peer
    And read the page of Wrong and Fate.

Pure matters I began to preach
    Of Righteousness and Love Atoning ;
The neighbours ran to hear, and each
    Was eager who'd begin . . . the stoning.

I scattered ashes on my head,
    The beggars' road from town I trod :
In the wilderness I make my bed,
    And get my meat, like birds, from God.

Keeping the Eternal's covenant,
   All things of earth obey and love me ;
Stars to my service ministrant
   Sparkle with frolic lamps above me.

But if with furtive hurrying feet
   I slip through town amid the noise,
I see the smile of self-conceit,
   And hear the old men tell the boys :

" Look ! Here was Pride — be warned and dread it ! —
   Would none of us to dwell among :
This fool would have his neighbours credit
   That God gave utterance to his tongue.

" Look well, you children. There he goes —
   Haggard and sour and bad and grim !
Look, he's no money, he's no clothes !
   And how they all think scorn of him ! "

                (J. S. PHILLIMORE)

Dream

By hot noon, in a vale of Dargestan,
Lifeless, a bullet in my breast, I lay ;
Smoke rose from a deep wound, and my blood ran
Out of me, drop by drop, and ebbed away.

I lay upon the burning sand alone.
Sheer precipices crowded all around.
Their yellow tops were scorching in the sun,
And I scorched too, in death's sleep, on the ground.

I dreamed a dream, and saw the glittering hours
Of evening gaiety in my own place ;
And there young women, garlanded with flowers,
Held talk of me in words of happy grace.

But in that happy talk not joining, one
Sat far apart, and sunk in thought she seemed ;
And oh ! — the cause is known to God alone —
This was the sad dream that her young soul dreamed.

She dreamed she saw a vale of Dargestan. . . . .
There on the slope a well-known body lay ;
Smoke rose from a black wound, and the blood ran
In cold streams out of it, and ebbed away.

(ANON.)

Gratitude

For all, for all, my thanks to Thee I offer,
For passion's martyrdom that no one knew,
For poisoned kisses, for the griefs I suffer,
Vengeance of foes, slander of friends untrue,
For the soul's ardour squandered in waste places,
For everything in life that cheated me, —
But see that now and after such Thy grace is
That I no longer must give thanks to Thee !

(C. M. BOWRA)

ALEXEY TOLSTOY
(1817–1875)

LAND of mine, where I was bred,
   Horses wildly flying,
Eagles screeching overhead,
   On the fields wolves crying !

Hail, dear land of my delight,
   Pinewoods thickly growing,
Nightingales that sing at sight,
   Steppe and cloud and blowing !

                 (C. M. BOWRA)

IT was an early day of spring,
The grass was scarcely showing,
Brooks ran, no heat was hovering,
And green the wood was glowing.

The shepherd to the morning breeze
Was not yet piping highly,
And still in curls among the trees
The fern was peeping shyly.

It was an early day of spring,
Beneath the birch-tree's cover ;
I saw your eyelids lowering,
I saw your sweet smile hover.

So to my love you made reply,
To me your glances drooping —
O life ! O wood ! O sunny sky !
O youth ! O happy hoping !

I burst in tears with wondering
Your sweet face to discover —
It was an early day of spring,
Beneath the birch-tree's cover.

It was the morning of our days —
O happiness ! O crying !
O wood ! O life ! O sunny rays !
O cool the birch-tree's sighing !

(C. M. BOWRA)

BELIEVE me not, friend, when in grief's unreason
I tell you that I love you now no more.
When the tide ebbs, believe not the sea's treason ;
It will come back, in loving, to the shore.

I love you still, with my old passion glowing ;
My freedom I shall give to you again.
Already waves with homeward sound are flowing
To coasts they love, back from the distant main.

(C. M. BOWRA)

WHERE boughs above the pool are swinging,
Where the hot summer sunshine burns,
The dragon-flies in airy winging
Lead on the dance's merry turns.

" Come hither, child, come nigh and hear us ;
For we shall teach you how to fly !
Come hither, child, come hither, near us,
And leave your mother slumb'ring by.

" Beneath us all the rushes tremble ;
All is so warm and happy here.
Our backs the turquoise-stone resemble,
Our glassy wings are crystal-clear.

" The songs we know to sing are many,
And we have loved you long ago.
Look at the bank more soft than any,
Look at the sandy floor below ! "

(ANON.)

A WELL, and the cherry-trees blowing,
The marks of a girl's naked foot,
And there, at the side of them showing,
The print of a hobnailed boot.

All is hushed at the place of their meeting;
But my ears jealous echoes assail,
The whispers, the passionate greeting,
The splash and the noise of the pail.

(C. M. BOWRA)

IT chanced when the dance was pealing,
In the whirl of the crowd's vain din,
I saw your face, but concealing
Mystery closed it in.

With sadness your eyes were filling;
But your voice rang such wonders to me,
Like the noise of a far pipe's trilling,
Like a foaming wave of the sea.

Your slender form gave me pleasure,
And the thoughtful look on your face;
But your laughter's mournful measure
Still in my heart has a place.

In the hours of the night, when lonely
And weary I lie on my bed,
I see your sad eyes only,
I hear your gay voice in my head.

I fall to sleep sadly, and flowing
Fancies unknown I see.
Do I love you? There is no knowing,
But it seems to be love to me.

(C. M. BOWRA)

In the leaves the raindrops gently
Dripped, and the rain had gone by.
Gently the trees shook in whispers,
Far off was a cuckoo's cry.

The moon looked out of a raincloud
As if through a mist of tears ;
I sat by a maple dreaming,
Dreaming of long lost years.

In those years I cannot be certain
That my soul was unsullied and true ;
But much then did not allure me,
And much then I would not do.

To-day I have made acquaintance
With wickedness, fraud and lies ;
And many a noble vision,
One after the other, flies.

I mused thus on days departed,
On days when I did not fail, —
In the leaves of the lofty maple
Above sang a nightingale.

It sang with so tender a passion,
As if this were its refrain :
" Take comfort, lament not vainly ;
That time will be yours once again."

(C. M. BOWRA)

Do you remember, Mary,
A house of bygone times,
And round a pond that slumbered
The immemorial limes ?

The overgrown old garden,
The silent walks and trees,
The lengthy row of portraits
Beneath the hall's high frieze ?

Do you remember, Mary,
The sky at eventime,
The endless level landscape,
The distant village chime?

The bank behind the garden,
The river's quiet flow,
The shimmering of the cornfields
Where coloured corn-flowers grow?

The wood where we the first time
Went wandering, you and I?
Do you remember, Mary,
The days that have passed by?

(HON. M. BARING)

OUTSIDE it is blowing and raining,
And all are asleep long ago;
I look with a sigh through the window
At the ghost of a garden I know.

The sky is but darkness, and darkness,
Not a star, not a glimmer of light,
And the old Manor House is so mournful
While it blows and it rains in the night.

The rain on the roof-tops is drumming,
The chandeliers tinkle and shake,
In the wallpaper next to the cupboard
The scurrying mice are awake;

They scent for themselves new abundance:
Soon the Master will die of decline,
The heir will abandon the Manor,
Where lived his illustrious line,

And the house will for ever be empty,
The overgrown steps out of sight . . .
And to think about this is so mournful
While it blows and it rains in the night.

(HON. M. BARING)

THROUGH the slush and the ruts of the highway,
  By the side of the dam of the stream,
Where the fishermen's nets are a-drying,
  The carriage jogs on, and I dream.

I dream, and I look at the highway,
  At the sky that is sullen and grey,
At the lake with its shelving reaches,
  And the curling smoke far away.

By the dam, with a cheerless visage,
  Walks a Jew who is ragged and sere;
With a thunder of foam and of splashing
  The waters race over the weir;

A boy over there is whistling
  On a hemlock flute of his make;
And the wild ducks get up in a panic
  And call as they sweep from the lake;

And near the old tumbling-down mill-house
  Some labourers sit on the ground;
With a sack-laden wagon a cart-horse
  Plods past with a lazy sound. . . .

It all seems to me so familiar,
  Although I have never been here,
The roof of that house out yonder,
  And the boy, and the wood, and the weir.

And the voice of the grumbling mill-wheel,
  And that mouldering barn I know,
I have been here and seen this already,
  And forgotten it all long ago.

The very same cart-horse was dragging
  Those sacks with the very same sound,
And those very same labourers sitting
  By the rickety mill on the ground;

And that Jew with the beard walked past me,
    And those waters raced over the weir —
Yes, all this has happened already,
    But I cannot tell when or where. . . .

(Hon. M. Baring)

The Convicts

The sun on the steppes is sinking,
And gold is the distant grass.
The convicts' fetters are clinking
On the dusty road as they pass.

They march, with heads closely shaven,
With heavy steps onward go,
Grief on their brows engraven
And doubt in their hearts below.

They march, with the shadows growing;
Two sorry beasts drag a cart,
And, lazily with them going,
Is a guard who lingers apart.

" Now, brothers, what of a chorus ?
Forget all our fortunes forlorn !
Disaster was written for us
Long ago when we were born."

Then they start up a tune together,
And try it, and break into song,
Of lazy days in fine weather,
Of the Volga that flows far and long.

Of freedom and steppes they are singing ;
They sing of an untamed will.
The day grows darker, and ringing
On the road the fetters clink still.

(C. M. Bowra)

Troparion

WHAT joy does earthly life possess
That hath no part in earthly sorrow ?
What joy that proves not false to-morrow ?
Where among men is happiness ?
Of all that we through toil obtain
Nothing is lasting, all is vain —
What glories on the earth are sure
And steadfast and unchanged endure ?
All is but shadow, dream, and sand,
And like a whirlwind blows away,
And face to face with Death we stand
Unarmed in helpless disarray.
The right-hand of the mighty one
Is nothing, naught the king's command —
Lord, now Thy servant's life is done,
Receive him in Thy blessèd land.

Death like a warrior hot with pride
Waylaid, and like a robber felled me,
The grave its jaws hath opened wide,
From all that liveth hath withheld me.
Be saved, my children and my kin,
From the grave hear my warning knell,
Brothers and friends, be saved from sin
So you escape the flames of hell.
Life is but vanity throughout
And, at the scent of death's decay,
Like unto flowers we fade away —
Why do we vainly toss about ?
The grave is what was once a throne,
Our palaces a heap of sand —
Lord, now Thy servant's life is done,
Receive him in Thy blessèd land.

Who midst the bones in rotting heap
Is warrior, judge, or king, or slave ?
Who shall be numbered with the sheep,
Who the rejected evil knave ?

Where is the silver and the gold,
O Brothers, where the hosts of slaves ?
And who among the nameless graves
The rich and poor beneath the mould ?
All is but smoke and dust and ash,
A dream, a shade, a phantom flash —
Lord, but in Thy bright Paradise
Our refuge and salvation lies.
All that was flesh beneath the sun
Shall rot, our pomps shall rot in sand —
Lord, now Thy servant's life is done,
Receive him in Thy blessèd land.

And Thou who for the world dost weep,
Thou, Advocate of the oppressed,
We cry to Thee, the Holiest,
For him, our brother here asleep.
Pray to Thy God-begotten Son,
Pray, O most pure of womankind,
That now our brother's life is done
He leave his sorrow here behind.
All is but smoke, and dust, and wraith,
O friends, in phantoms put no faith !
When we upon some sudden day
Shall scent the breath of death's decay,
We shall be stricken every one,
Like corn beneath the reaper's hand —
Lord, now Thy servant's life is done,
Receive him in Thy blessèd land.

I travel on a road unknown,
Half hopeful, half in fear I go.
My sight is dim, my heart a stone,
My lids are sealed, my hearing slow,
And motionless, bereft of speech,
I cannot hear the brethren wail.
And out of sight and out of reach
The censer's blue and fragrant veil ;
But till in endless sleep I fall,
My love shall never pass away,
And by that love I, brethren, pray

That each thus unto God shall call :
Lord, on that day when moon and sun
Shall vanish at the trump's command —
Now that Thy servant's life is done,
Receive him in Thy blessèd land.

(HON. M. BARING)

YAKOV POLONSKY
(1819–1898)

The Blind Preacher

Upon a lonely road at shut of day
   Bede, the blind preacher, leaning on a lad
   To stay his steps, barefoot — what clothes he had
Fluttering loose in the breeze — took his rough way.

More grisly grew the inhuman wild, and blank :
   Nothing but here a pine-trunk, ages old,
   There a grey boulder jutting from the mould,
Bearded with shaggy moss and lichens dank.

The lad was tired. Perhaps a bush in reach
   Showed tempting berries ; or, for the mere jest,
   To fool the blind — " I'll go," says he, " to rest,
And now's your time if you've a mind to preach.

" Shepherds have seen us from the high hillside ;
   Women are here expecting, children hem
   The path, grey elders — speak of God to them,
And of His son for our sins crucified."

A sudden glamour lit the age-worn face.
   As springs rock-bound upbursting crack their shell,
   So from his wan lips burst the living well
Of inspiration, like a torrent race.

He spoke as faith can speak. The blind man seemed
   To read the Apocalypse behind the skies :
   Heavenward his frail head beckoned prophet-wise ;
Tears in his disillumined sockets gleamed.

.   .   .   .

Look ! now the pale moon drops behind the hill ;
   The red gold in the East begins to kindle ;
   Night vapours deep in valley bottoms dwindle. . . .
But when the Saint in rapture, preaching still,

F

Felt his arm nudged, and heard the laughing boy's
" Enough !   There's no one left — let's on again,"
   And ceased, bowing his head in silence, — then
All round with vast and congregated noise
   The stones of the wilderness returned " Amen ".

                (J. S. PHILLIMORE)

The Swan

THE quaver'd plea of the fiddle ; gardens glowing
   With sudden flares : a to-and-fro of crowds :
All other things awake, but no wind blowing
   Under the roof of night to unpack the clouds.

Beneath blind heavens a blind green pool, whereon,
   Sequestered by the reeds from human eye,
In the merciful dusk a wounded swan
   Obscurely agonising waits to die.

So near quite spent, he cared no more to mark
   (His misanthropic shyness grown so tame)
How jetting rockets tore the veil of dark
   And o'er him broke the beads of sprinkled flame.

Nor cared to hear the pulse of the slow stream,
   Or soft discoursing of a neighbour fount :
His eyes fast shut, his brain is all a dream
   Of mounting high beyond where clouds can mount.

Ah, what a fugue shall launch his wing,
   Sky-rover enfranchised of glory !
And ah ! the song, the song he'll sing
   In the empyrean auditory !

His inmost, holiest meditation,
   Untuned for man — a swan 'mid swans ;
And kindred throats of his white nation
   Shall echo him in antiphons.

A moment more — it comes ! it comes ! —
　And the large freedom-song is born :
His beating vans (they stir !) like drums
　Salute the approaches of the morn !

— So fared his trance.　But not a feather stirr'd ;
　The imagined notes ebbed falteringly away.
With flights unflown and song unsung, the bird
　Died in the fitful darkness where he lay.

A bush trembled ;　the reeds half waved asunder
　To let a breath of air steal through the middle :
The garden grinned and coruscated under
　An ink-black sky ;　and quavering went the fiddle.

(J. S. Phillimore)

AFANASI FET
(1820–1892)

STORM in the skies in the evening,
Noise of the wrath of the sea ;
Storm on the sea, and the thronging
Thoughts that are torture to me ;

Storm on the sea, and insurgent
Thoughts that are clamorous in me,
Cloud after cloud flying blackly,
Noise of the wrath of the sea.

(O. ELTON)

WHAT an evening ! Streamlets run,
    Banks are breaking,
Nightingales in set of sun
    Music making.

Moonbeams from on high invade,
    Flood the fallows ;
In the gully willows' shade,
    Gleam of shallows.

There's an old leak in the weir,
    Planks are failing ;
Dangerously lean you here
    On the railing.

So to new life everything
    Spring delivers ;
Every field and copse must sing
    As it quivers.

Like these choirs, we shall be dumb,
    Cease from singing ;
But our children then will come,
    Carols ringing.

Not they only, — grandsons too
    With a chorus ;
With the spring to earth will flow
    Tunes sonorous.

(C. M. Bowra)

Swallows

On nature ever idly spying,
Forgetting all around, I'm fond
Of watching arrowy swallows flying,
When evening comes, above the pond.

See there a swallow darting, scratching
The glassy surface, till I fear
The alien element will be catching
The wings that swift as lightning veer.

Again that confident elation,
Again dark water flowing by . . .
Is it not such, my inspiration ?
And, among human beings, I ?

Seek I not thus a way forbidden,
I, vessel made of earthen clay,
Who search for something strange and hidden
And yearn to scoop a drop away ?

(Anon.)

The Prisoner

By bars of my prison
    The thick nettle lies ;
A willow has risen
    Pavilion-wise.

Boats gaily are seeking
    The far-away blue ;
The lattice is creaking,
    My file passes through.

My sorrowful dreaming
Is quiet in me ;
The waters are gleaming,
I soon shall be free.

No gloom my heart darkens,
My ache is at rest ;
And while my ear hearkens,
Hand files with a zest.

(C. M. Bowra)

To the Stars that have gone out

Curious eyes of those blue skyey spaces,
Tell me how long shall your glimmer inspire me ?
Long shall I feel, that in night's holy places
Nothing is nobler or fairer to fire me.

Quenched in some era forgotten, you may be
Nothing at all, though you still flame afar there ;
— This dead man's songs to you flying, shall they be
The ghost of a sign to the ghost of a star there ?

(O. Elton)

Whispering.   A timid sigh.
A nightingale that trills.
Silver, and a lullaby
From the unseen rills.

Twilight with a deepening blue.
Darkness falls apace.
Beauty yields to beauties new
On her enchanted face.

Roses when the greyness clears,
That amber drives away.
And love, and love again, and tears,
And the break of day.

(R. M. Hewitt)

For long I stood motionless, watching
  Stars and still more stars beyond,
And there seemed to grow up in the stillness
  Between me and the stars a bond.

I thought . . . something I have forgotten. . . .
  Far music I heard faintly chime ;
Very gently the stars were swaying. . . .
  I have loved the stars since that time.

(V. DE S. PINTO)

All, all that once was mine is mine for ever.
  Time cannot fetter dreams. The spirit is free,
And, in its blissful visions, cannot sever
  Young dreams from old ; they all are one to me.

A ray of momentary hope flits wreathing
  Beyond the dull fixed shores of everyday ;
The spirit in the body's forge is seething,
  Yet on her wandering wings still flies away.

No word of joy or freedom sounds to save me
  Yonder, where iron fate is lord of all.
Come hither ! How shall Nature here enslave me
  When she herself is nothing but my thrall ?

(O. ELTON)

Never

I am awake. . . . A coffin-lid. . . . I strain
To lift my hands from it in violent shaking.
I cry for help. I call to mind the pain
That I endured at death, — but now I'm waking !
Like cobwebs, easily the lid unrolled
I push aside, and leave my house of mould.

I stand, — all blinded by the gleaming snow.
Beyond all doubting, breaks the vault asunder.

I see the frost. No door keeps me below.
I shall go home. How great will be the wonder!
I know the park. I cannot miss the way.
But strange it looks to me, and changed, to-day. . . .

I run through snow. Into the air profound
Stretch unmoved boughs from trees decayed and hoary;
No track, no echo. Silence all around,
As in Death's kingdom in a world of story.
There is the house. . . . In desolation, all!
My outstretched arms in stupefaction fall.

The village sleeps in a dumb sheet of snow,
By endless, pathless, desolate plains surrounded.
Yes, so it is! That distant hill I know,
The church on it where once the bells' peal sounded.
And as a traveller, dead and frozen, lies,
It shows its outline to the cloudless skies.

Upon the snow no moth, no winter bird.
I see it all! The earth has long been cold
And dead. Then, why should still be heard
Breath in my breast? Why did the grave unfold
To give me back again? My consciousness
Is bound — to what? and what does it confess?

Nowhere to go, and no one to embrace,
Where Time has vanished into endless vastness!
O Death, return, and gather the last trace
Of life's predestined burden to thy fastness!
And thou, Earth's frozen body, onward fly
And take my corpse into eternity!

(C. M. BOWRA)

NIKOLAY NEKRASOV
(1821–1877)

Home

BEHOLD it once again, the old familiar place,
Wherein my fathers passed their barren, vacant days !
In muddy revels ran their lives, in witless bragging,
In little bullying ways, in gluttonies unflagging ;
The swarm of shivering serfs in their oppression found
An enviable thing the master's meanest hound ;
And here to see the light of heaven I was fated,
And here I learned to hate, and bear the thing I hated ;
But all my hate I hid within my soul for shame,
And I at seasons too a yokel squire became ;
And here it was my soul, untimely spoilt and tainted,
With blessed rest and peace too soon was disacquainted ;
Unchildish trouble then, and premature desires,
Lay heavy on my heart, and scorched it with their fires.
The days of a man's youth in memory, 'tis notorious,
Are like a sumptuous dream, are trumpeted as glorious ;
— Those beauteous memories file in order before me,
Only to fill my heart with anger and ennui.

Here is the dark, dark close.   See, where the branches thicken
What figure glimpses down the pathway, sad and stricken ?
Too well the cause I know, my mother, of thy tears ;
Too well I know who marred and wasted all thy years.
For ever doomed to serve a sullen churl untender,
Unto no hopeless hope thy spirit would surrender ;
To no rebellious dream thy timorous heart was stirred ;
Thy lot, like any serf's, was borne without a word.
No frigid soul was thine, I know, or void of passion,
But resolute, and framed in proud and lovely fashion ;
And all the wrongs that still thy ebbing strength could bear
Thy last faint words forgave thy slayer, watching there !
And thou, too, with that sad mute sufferer partaking
Her dreadful lot, and all the outrage and the aching,
Thou also art no more, my heart's own sister, mine !
Out of those doors by cur and servile concubine

69

Infested, thou must flee from shame unto disaster,
Commit thy lot unto a strange, an unloved master,
Aye, and rehearse afar the doom that fell on her,
Thy mother. Even he, the executioner,
Shuddered before thy bier, was once betrayed to weeping,
To see thee with that smile so cold and rigid sleeping.

— Now it is blind and blank, that mansion old and grey ;
Women and dogs, buffoons and lackeys, where are they ?
Gone ; but, of old, I know not what oppression leaden
Weighed upon great and small, the weary heart to deaden.
— Unto the nurse I fled. But ah ! the nurse ! how smarted
The tears I wept for her, when all too heavy-hearted !
To hear her name may stir the springs of old emotion,
But long, how long ! has been extinct my heart's devotion ;
Chance memories arise to trace and trace again
How her insensate love and kindness were my bane ;
And lo ! my heart again with wrath and rancour swelling !

Nay, from those younger years of harshness and rebelling
No recollection brings one comfortable ray ;
But all that from the first ensnared my life, and lay
Upon me like a ban irrevocably blasting,
All, all began at home, in this my birthplace.   Casting
My gaze in loathing round, it gives me comfort still
To see that they have felled the dark pinewood, the chill
Shelter for tired men from summer heats reposing ;
The fallows are burnt up, the herds are idly dozing
And hang their heads above the streamlet parched with drought ;
The crazy mansion, void and sullen, bulges out,
Where once the long dull note of stifled lamentation
Chimed with the clash of cups and shouts of exultation ;
Where he who ground the rest beneath him — only he
To live his life, or act, or draw his breath, was free.

(O. ELTON)

The Unreaped Field

IT grows late Autumn, and the rooks are flown ;
   The woods are bare ; all empty stands the plain ;
One field is yet unreaped, one field alone.
   It sets me musing in a mournful train.

Surely these cornstalks whisper one to the other :
  " This Autumn wind, it has a weary sound ;
And weary work it is to sink and smother
  Good grain in dust by bending tops to ground.

" The mighty havoc of these wild horse-droves !
  The hares that trample us down, the squalls that batter !
The toll to every robber-beak that roves ! . . .
  Where is the goodman tarrying ? What's the matter ?

" Are we so worse a plant than all the rest ?
  Blade, bloom and grain — what found he to mislike ?
Nay, 'tis not that ; we're buxom at the best :
  Long since the full ear plumped the nodding spike.

" Was it for this he ploughed and sowed the piece,
That autumn winds should scatter our increase ? "

A doleful answer on the winds comes blowing :
  " He's no more man to do the work you ask.
He meant not this at ploughing time or sowing,
  Nor reckoned strength should fail him for his task.

" He cannot eat or drink — the worm so burrows
  And sucks his heart that now poor Gaffer's lips
Refuse him food ; the hands which traced your furrows
  Are limp as any thong and shrunk to chips ;

" His eyes too bleared to see ; the voice quite spent
  Which sang his melancholy thought aloud
While gripping the ash-tail hard, the old yeoman went
  Ploughing and meditating as he ploughed."

(J. S. PHILLIMORE)

The Hungry One

THE peasant stands
With haggard gaze,
He pants for breath,
He reels and sways ;

From famine food,
From bread of bark,
His form has swelled,
His face is dark.

Through endless grief
Suppressed and dumb
His eyes are glazed,
His soul is numb.

As though in sleep,
With footsteps slow,
He creeps to where
The rye doth grow.

Upon his field
He gazes long,
He stands and sings
A voiceless song :

" Grow ripe, grow ripe,
O Mother Rye,
I fostered thee,
Thy lord am I.

" Yield me a loaf
Of monstrous girth,
A cake as vast
As Mother Earth.

" I'll eat the whole —
No crumb I'll spare ;
With wife, with child,
I will not share."

(JULIET M. SOSKICE)

OH tread not the road
So shining and broad :

Along it there speed
With feverish tread
The multitudes led
By infamous greed.

There lives which are spent
With noble intent
Are mocked at in scorn ;
There souls lie in chains,
And bodies and brains
By passions are torn,

By animal thirst
For pleasures accurst
Which pass in a breath.
There hope is in vain,
For there is the reign
Of darkness and death.

In front of your eyes
Another road lies —
'Tis honest and clean.
Though steep it appears
And sorrow and tears
Upon it are seen :

It leads to the door
Of those who are poor,
Who hunger and thirst,
Who pant without air,
Who die in despair —
Oh, there be the first !

(Juliet M. Soskice)

The Wife's Lament

My life is like daytime
With no sun to warm it !
My life is like night
With no glimmer of moon !

73

And I — the young woman —
Am like the swift steed
On the curb, the young swallow
With wings crushed and broken;
My jealous old husband
Is drunken and snoring,
But even while snoring,
He keeps one eye open,
And watches me always,
Me, poor little wife!

(JULIET M. SOSKICE)

GOOD-BYE! Forget the days of wane,
Dejection, bitterness and pain,
Forget the storms, forget the tears,
Forget the threats of jealous fears.
But the days when the sun of love
Uprising kissed us from above,
And bravely we went on our way —
Bless and forget not one such day.

(HON. M. BARING)

APOLLON MAYKOV
(1821–1897)

Pan

HE sleeps, he slumbers —
The great Pan sleeps !
The glare of noon
Engrossing him cumbers
The great god's brain.
There breathe from heaps
Of ripely sunn'd grasses
Spells which solicit
Again and again,
Till drowsiness passes
Withstanding. He slumbers :
Profuse dreams visit
His deep-tranced swoon.

The roe-deer, panting,
Lies couched in the brake :
Her eye scarce peeps.
Of flock and of herd
The least sounds fail.
On the sward lies the snake,
Not stirring a scale.
In the wood, no bird
But ceases descanting :
The tree-top numbers
Are mute — no word !
He sleeps, he slumbers —
The great Pan sleeps !

With sultry hum
Of beetles and bees,
Near to him dangles
A come-go-and-come
Of orbits and spangles ;
A shimmering swarm.
And aloft o'er these

A fugue of sunn'd pigeons,
Cross-cruising, white-bladed,
They glide, they glance,
Ravelling, unravelling,
In rapid manœuvre. . . .
Below, Pan sleeps.
Still higher, brigaded
In sharp wedge-form,
What host has invaded —
What white host sweeps
Yon aeriest regions ?
The cranes advance !
The cranes, far-travelling,
Advance and pass over !

In the supreme temple
Whose blue veil man
Sees not nor sunders
The watchers assemble
To guard his sleep.
Half heard they keep
Watch over the deep
Slumber of Pan :
And he dreams wonders. . . .
To his dreams it seems
He scans unhind'red
Where Olympus discloses
His heaven-born kindred.
The gods' mount glisters,
And down sky-steeps
Goddesses his sisters
Scatter like roses
Sweet dreams past number —
Handfuls of dreams
For the great god's slumber,
The sleep Pan sleeps.

Tread tiptoe, Child,
And break not his rest !
Nay, stir not, but rather
Sit here in a nest

Where tall weeds darken
And deep grass wreathes ;
Sit quiet and hearken —
His sleep, how mild !
How softly he breathes !

And so from aloft,
From the most high heaven,
So meek, so soft,
The dreams shall gather,
And o'er us creep, —
The sorrow-benumbers,
The healers of man,
The dreams that leaven
The great Pan's sleep.

He sleeps, he slumbers,
The great god Pan !

(J. S. PHILLIMORE)

IVAN SURIKOV
(1841–1880)

Ukrainian Song

In a meadow by the roadway
   Corn is growing deep :
Comes a maiden to the meadow
   Yellow corn to reap.

Hands are tired and feet are aching
   For that girl so fair. . . .
My beloved, my bright falcon,
   Where are you, oh where ?

Come to me, my heart's desire,
   Oh come back again.
See, the golden ears of wheat
   Ripen on the plain.

Warm the corn beneath the sunshine,
   Bright sky overhead :
For your sake, my little falcon,
   Many tears are shed.

(V. DE S. PINTO)

In the green garden the nightingale
   Her happy music is making,
But I who am still so young
   Have a heart in my breast that's breaking.

You must know since I was christened
   Fate dealt me an evil measure :
All her beauty my mother gave me —
   It was her only treasure.

With her I grew up and was cherished,
   Through childhood happily gliding ;
" Pretty maid " rich merchants called me,
   As past us they came riding.

My little cheeks were rosy :
   They glowed when play had fired them ;
My tresses were long and yellow,
   All the village admired them.

Then my father ruined my life :
   To a rich old man he took me,
To wed a grey-bearded old man !
   Then all my joy forsook me.

I can't live with him ; I am wretched.
   With grief my heart is breaking,
A bitter rain of tears
   The rose from my cheeks is taking.

What are riches to me without joy ?
   Life without love is past bearing.
I am young, yet before my time
   I have grown old and despairing.

(V. DE S. PINTO

VLADIMIR SOLOVYEV
(1853–1900)

Do you not see, Beloved ?
All that about us lies
Is but the shade, the mirrored image
Of things not seen with eyes.

Do you not hear, Beloved ?
The sounds that to earth belong
Are but the muffled and broken echo
Of a noble triumph-song.

Do you not feel, Beloved ?
Our joy that will not end —
The joy of a silent love-greeting
That friend bestows on friend.

(R. M. Hewitt)

Once in the misty dawn with timid foot
Towards a mysterious shrine I walked alone ;
   The stars were paling in the eastern light,
   My soul engaged the host of dreams in fight
And prayed to gods unknown.

Now in the cold hard light I tread as then
A lonely path, beside an unknown stream ;
   The mists are fled, and clearly shows by day
   How rough the mountain-track, how far away
The haven of my dream.

But till the midnight hour with fearless foot
I travel to the goal of my desires ;
   Where on the summit, 'neath an alien star,
   Along the sacred roof will gleam afar
The line of victory-fires.

(R. M. Hewitt)

INNOKENTI ANNENSKI
(1856–1909)

A Minute

WHEN a patterned stuff will so flutter,
And a burning flame is so white,
No need now to smile or to utter :
Just remain as you were, in my sight.

Just remain in your darkness and drooping,
More pale than an autumn at dawn,
Out there where the willow is stooping
To shivering shadows of lawn.

A minute — the wind will come shaking
The leaves into patterns around.
A minute — the heart then awaking
Will know 'tis not you that it found.

Just stay then, and smile not nor utter ;
Just stay as a vision so long
As a patterned stuff will so flutter
And a white burning flame is so strong.

(C. M. BOWRA)

My Anguish

LET vain excitement's shrine be covered with new grasses,
And let the waxen hand be in the grave forgot.
Naught but confusion will be all my life that passes
With you, it seems, and anguished longing all my lot.

No, not for those alas ! to whom, so undeserving,
I did in jealous care and passion once belong.
Oh calm of lovers' strength, even in grief not swerving,
Oh woman's tenderness so enviably strong !

Since this is so, why should confusion round me gather?
No, love is radiant; it is as crystal — air. . . .
Mine, being Unlove, shivers like a horse in lather:
She gives a poisoned feast, a feast with swindling fare.

In garlands of azaleas that fade and wither
She sought a song. . . . She saw not her first line arise,
Before they tied her little children's limbs together
And broke their hands in pieces and made blind their eyes.

She has no sex. On all alike her lips are playing;
She's a dissembler, and she has a vicious taste.
She spends the livelong day an empty cradle swaying —
Sweet Jesus! in the corner see her image placed!

I made her, — yet she is a vision, not delusion!
I love her not at all, — and she is near to me;
She is herself confused, and she is my confusion,
Always delighted, yet my anguished longing she!

(C. M. BOWRA)

FEDOR SOLOGUB
(1863–1927)

God, who created me from sodden clay,
  Has from the earth not set me free.
All that my earth, its dales and peaks display,
  As my own self, is dear to me.

When to a distant road my glances flit,
  It seems to me I understand
All rolling wheels, all stones and steps on it,
  As if I held them in my hand.

When I behold a sounding torrent's course,
  It seems to me that it must bring
Earth's sap to me, and its life-giving force,
  And give it to my spring.

(C. M. Bowra)

When over the river mists blow,
By the moon on a lonely night,
They fill me with hatred, they fill with delight;
Such quiet is in them, such woe.

I forget all the beauty of day,
In the mist I silently pace;
A scarce visible path in my trouble I trace,
With a burden of lonely despair on my way.

(Anon.)

She was in a village by a forest side,
She knocked at the doors and loudly she cried . . .
It was growing dark; she was terrified.
The grim doors were shut, and entrance was denied.

For a long, long time she wandered far and wide.
Oh lonely it was in the darkness to abide

With grim doors shut and entrance denied,
And darkness threatening like a rising tide !

When triumphant morning in all its pride
Rose on the world, she had fallen, she had died.

(V. DE S. PINTO)

Lullaby in Undertones

RUNNING barefoot all the day,
    Time for him to go to bed.
We must wash the dust away,
    While he droops his little head.
I will sing, and all for you,
Bayú-bayushki-bayú.

Who is tapping at the door ?
    I can guess. It's only Sleep.
Hair of flax and hand of wax,
    Not the little chimney-sweep.
Softly now I sing for you,
Bayushki-bayú.

Where've you been, Sleep ? Over hill.
    What to see ? The Moon was bright.
All alone ? My sister too.
    Brought her with you ? Not to-night.
Gently now I sing to you,
Bayushki-bayú.

Drowsy Moon is weak and pale,
    Far above us in the sky.
Someone at the window-sill
    Murmurs, murmurs, " Here am I."
Very low I sing to you,
Bayushki-bayú.

Someone murmurs at the sill,
    Like the rustling of a bough,

" I am very faint and ill.
   Help me, brother, help me now."
Lower yet I sing to you,
Bayushkí-bayú.

" I've been mowing all the day,
   I am tired, I am ill."
Flits a shade across the pane,
   Hides below the window-sill.
But I sing, and all for you,
Bayú-bayushkí-bayú.

(R. M. HEWITT)

VYACHESLAV IVANOV
(1866–   )

Beauty's Nomads

WIDE acres you inherit,
And graveyards populous ;
A tameless nomad spirit
Is Beauty's fate for us.

For us a daily treason,
New camp-grounds every day.
The inexorable prison
We cheat, and break away.

Trust in each shrouded story,
Each far-off marvel's prize,
The springtime's emerald glory,
The length and breadth of skies.

Artists, with dreams for horses,
Pasture them all around !
Escape ! Sow with new forces,
Then fly the fallow ground.

Hurl from your flooding numbers
Your hordes in hurricanes
Where the low valley slumbers
And slaves are proud of chains.

Trample their paradises,
Attila ! Waste anew !
And where your bright star rises,
The steppe will bud for you !

(C. M. BOWRA)

Complaint

THY soul, unhearing and unspeaking,
In its dark forest droops to sleep,
Where droves of dark desires are breaking
And through the tangled brushwood sweep.

To guide thee where the stars are keeping
My home, I made a flame burn bright ;
In empty brake, in forest sleeping,
I sowed the torch's seed of light.

I shine, I cry to pathless spaces ;
In silence the numb thickets brood.
Neither with men nor God thy place is,
Soul, hidden in thy solitude.

(C. M. BOWRA)

The Road to Emmaus

Now has the third day's red sail come
To haven on its westering way ;
In the soul — Golgotha, the tomb,
Dispute, and riot, and dismay.

And craftily, the cruel night
Stands everywhere on sentinel,
And though the warming sun is bright,
It has not strength the dark to quell.

Death, the inexorable, gapes ;
The heart is stifled in the grave . . .
Somewhere are white and shining shapes,
Gold on the gloom, wrath on the wave !

And frenzied women, pale with tears,
Proclaim good tidings — but of what ?
From crushing and denying fears
The lulling mist lets nothing out.

Someone, a stranger, on the road,
Stopping to speak to us, proclaims
A sacrificed and a dead God . . .
And the heart breathes again, and flames.

(C. M. Bowra)

KONSTANTIN BALMONT
(1867–   )

I CAME into this world to see the sunlight,
   The skyline's sapphire glow,
I came into this world to see the sunlight,
   And peaks of snow.

I came into this world to see the ocean,
   The vale's rich flower-starred pall,
Mine eyes beheld a thousand worlds in motion,
   And conquered all.

I overcame oblivion with the trembling
   Dream-echoes of my lyre,
My heart is pure and free from all dissembling
   And full of fire.

I am beloved because mine accents ringing
   In suffering had their birth;
Who is my peer in the sweet art of singing?
   No man on earth.

I came into this world to see the sunlight,
   And if day ends its race,
I still shall sing the glory of the sunlight
   In death's embrace.

(W. MATTHEWS)

Life's Purpose

I ASKED of the unfettered breezes
How youth could be mine all my days;
And answered the frolicking breezes:
" Be thou airy as breezes, as haze ! "

I asked of the powerful ocean
What life's mighty purpose might be;
And answered the boisterous ocean:
" Be ever full-throated, like me ! "

I asked of the limitless sunshine
How to shine with the dawn's glowing light ;
No answer came back from the sunshine,
But my soul heard a whisper, " Burn bright ! "

(ANON.)

The Reeds

WHEN midnight has come to the desolate fen,
Almost unheard is the reeds' rustle then.

What do they whisper, and what do they say ?
Why are the marshlights among them at play ?

They glimmer and shimmer and vanish from sight ;
Then again is rekindled that wandering light.

When midnight has come, the reeds sway and shake ;
They shelter the toad and the hiss of the snake.

Over the marsh flits a face dying fast —
'Tis the lead-coloured moon who is sad and downcast.

In an odour of slime the mists stealthily creep . . .
The marshland entices, devours and sucks deep.

" But whom ? for what reason ? " the reeds seem to say,
" Why are the marshlights among us at play ? "

But the lead-coloured moon, who is sad and downcast,
Knows nothing and sinks till her face fades at last,

And the echoing sob of a soul as it dies
Rises up from the reeds in soft sorrowful sighs.

(C. M. BOWRA)

VALERI BRYUSOV
(1873–1924)

Orpheus and Eurydice

ORPHEUS

Ah, I hear your soft step treading,
Hear behind me your soft tread ;
A rebellious way we're threading,
Life's pale pathway from the dead.

EURYDICE

Yours to see, but mine to hearken ;
I must pace on, I must pace,
Though my face the black clouds darken,
Death's black veil upon my face.

ORPHEUS

Upward, upward, each step takes us
To the noise, the world, the sun ;
There the shadow's gloom forsakes us,
There my love will make us one.

EURYDICE

No, I dare not, no, I dare not,
Husband, brother, friend to me ;
I am a faint shadow ; stare not —
Just a shadow you will see.

ORPHEUS

Trust me. At the end awaited,
Like me, you shall greet the spring.
I, with God's lyre consecrated,
Songs of life for you shall sing.

EURYDICE

What can songs avail me, — knowing
Quiet that no words can tell ?
What is spring, — who knew the sowing
In the land of asphodel ?

ORPHEUS

Ah, remember the green meadows,
Laughing song and dancing feet,
Ah, remember secret shadows,
Hot embraces, shy and sweet!

EURYDICE

Dead my heart, my breast unshaken, —
How believe in your caress?
I remember sleep, — your spoken
Words, poor friend, are meaningless.

ORPHEUS

Not remember! You forget me!
Every moment I retrace.
Not the grave itself will let me
Be forgetful of your face.

EURYDICE

I recall, poor friend, sweet pleasure,
And love too, like gentle sleep . . .
But in darkness without measure
Your pale face I cannot keep.

ORPHEUS

Look at it!
        and Orpheus madly
Turns it to the empty black, —
And her name repeated, sadly
Through the shades re-echoes back.

(C. M. BOWRA)

The Stonecutter

— STONECUTTER, stonecutter, aproned in white,
What are you building? for whom?
— Hey, do not trouble us. We must build right.
From this a prison will come.

— Stonecutter, stonecutter, levelling true,
What man inside it will grieve?

— Neither your brother, O rich man, nor you ;
You'll never learn how to thieve.

— Stonecutter, stonecutter, who will it be
Weeps thro' the night wide-awake ?
— Maybe my son will, a workman like me.
Such is the load that we take.

— Stonecutter, stonecutter, will his thought rest
On them who built this before ?
— Hey, look, a ladder's no place for a jest !
We know it all.   Say no more.

(C. M. BOWRA)

Benediction

THE shining splendour of your eyes I bless !
It shone on the delirium that was mine.

The smile that lingers on your lips I bless !
For it has made me drunken as with wine.

The poison hidden in your kiss I bless !
Its venom drove my dreams and thoughts astray.

The sickle that is your embrace I bless !
It cut down all past things that in me lay.

The conflagration of your love I bless !
A pyre I kindled for it joyfully.

The darkness that is in your soul I bless !
It spread with mantling pinions over me.

For everything, for everything I bless !
For grief and ache and dread thro' days untold,

Because you drew me on to Paradise,
Because outside its gateway I am cold !

(C. M. BOWRA)

Two Voices

1ST VOICE

WHERE art thou, my darling ?
Lean down over me.
While I slept unfurling
Dark wings threatened me.
Night, with no dawn breaking,
Held me in its thrall,
And my heart was aching. . . .

2ND VOICE

I hear someone call.

1ST VOICE

Why art thou far parted ?
Void the air above ;
And my lips deserted
Seek the lips they love.
Why art thou not lying
In the bed with me ?
Whence art thou replying ?

2ND VOICE

In the grave with thee.

1ST VOICE

From the shroud's thick cover,
Hands and arms, begone !
Where art thou, my lover ?
Night will make us one.
Words of love repeating,
Unto thee I strive.
Where's thy kiss, thy greeting ?

2ND VOICE

Art thou still alive ?

1ST VOICE

Thou, I know, art nigh me
In this dark dumb place.

Bend thy dear head by me;
I will kiss thy face.
Has the night above thee
Made love disappear?
Lov'st thou as I love thee?

2ND VOICE

This is Heaven here.

(C. M. Bowra)

The Coming Huns

Oh, where are you, Huns, who are coming?
As a cloud you swell over us here.
I can hear iron footsteps a-drumming
On the yet undiscovered Pamir.

From your camps in the mist let the gathered
Hordes drunkenly fall in a flood;
Give new life to our bodies withered
With your free and fiery blood.

Obeying your unfettered spirit,
Set your tents as of old at our door,
And let the glad ploughland inherit
The hall where the throne stood before.

Pile up books for a conflagration
And dance in the gladdening light.
In the church do abomination, —
You are blameless as babes in men's sight.

And we who are wise men and singers,
Who protect hidden truth from the grave,
Will carry a flame that still lingers
In catacomb, desert and cave.

And what, when the hurricane's raving
In the murderous thunderstorm,
Will the gamester Chance be saving
From the secret shapes that we form?

Past tracking, may be, it will perish
What alone of the living we knew ;
But the death that you bring me I cherish,
And my hymns give a welcome to you !

(C. M. Bowra)

ALEXANDER BLOK
(1880–1921)

I HAVE forebodings of Thee.   Time is going, —
I fear for all that in Thy face I see.

The sky's aflame, intolerably glowing ;
Silent, I wait in love and agony.

The sky's aflame, draws near Thy apparition,
But it is strange.   Thy look will change on Thee.

And in me Thou dost wake a bold suspicion, —
Thy face will change from what it used to be.

How I shall fall ! how sorrowful and lowly,
Unmastered all my mortal fantasy !

The sky's aflame.   Draws near Thy splendour holy,
But it is strange.   Thy look will change on Thee.

(C. M. BOWRA)

A MAIDEN's song in the choir was telling
Of all who in far-off countries fret,
Of all ships that sail upon waters swelling,
Of all who their happiness forget.

So sang her voice, in the great dome soaring ;
On her pale white shoulders the gleam was bright,
And everyone in the dimness hearing
Saw a pale dress sing in the gleaming light.

And it seemed that near to them gladness hovered,
That in quiet rivers each ship was at rest,
That the weary people had discovered
In far-off lands the life of the blest.

The voice was sweet, and the light was throbbing ;
And only on high, at the Holy Door,
A child partook of the Mystery, sobbing
For one who would never come back to him more.

(ANON.)

Shadows on the Wall

THERE a king once went in dancing
Jaggèd diadem crowned.

Jester went in winged cloak, prancing
With his bells around,

Dames with pages and long trains
In the roses' shade,

Knight-at-arms, whose gloomy chains
On his steel limbs played.

Ah, for thy proud bearing, knight,
A long sword was meet !

Soft, beneath thy visor, knight,
Looks of love would greet !

Ah, a great cock's comb, my knight,
Made thy helmet gay !

Ah, but tell me, my sweet knight,
How thou cam'st this way ?

To my stories, my sweet knight,
Thy attention lend. . . .

See these roses, my sweet knight,
Given by a friend.

For she sent these roses, knight,
My sweet friend to me.

Ah, thou art a story, knight !
What's a rose to thee ?

(C. M. BOWRA)

Autumn Love

WHEN rowan leaves are dank and rusting
And rowan berries red as blood,
When in my palm the hangman's thrusting
The final nail with bony thud,

When, over the foul flooding river,
Upon the wet grey height, I toss
Before my land's grim looks, and shiver
As I swing here upon the cross,

Then, through the blood and weeping, stretches
My dying sight to space remote ;
I see upon the river's reaches
Christ sailing to me in a boat.

The same hopes in His eyes are dwelling,
From Him the self-same tatters trail,
And piteous from His garments swelling
His hand, as mine, pierced by the nail.

O Christ, how my own places grieve me !
Upon the cross I faint and die.
Oh will Thy boat yet come to save me
Where I am crucified on high ?

(C. M. BOWRA)

DEAD roses and dying
I carry alone ;
In frost, with snow flying,
I've far to be gone.
The same pathway treading,
Sword shouldered, he goes ;
He follows, and, spreading,
His cloak of mist flows.
He goes, and remembers
That snow I must tread,
That there the last embers
Of sunset are dead,

That I have unceasing
Toil all through the night,
That comes no releasing
To me from my plight.
And where, long delaying,
For sleep shall I go ?
Only roses are spraying
The soft melting snow,
Tears only are straying
On dark scarlet snow.
My anguish is nameless,
No help can I know.
But rose-blossoms, aimless,
He treads in the snow.

(C. M. BOWRA)

YOU say that I'm asleep, and you
Laugh over me, humiliating ;
And you would force me to repeating
A hundred times " My love is true ".

Your southern voice is soft, your grace
The grace of a gazelle recalling ;
But I come to you from a place
Of storm where endless snows are falling.

Strange the light valse's echoes seem ;
A stifling cloud above you lowers.
For me you are a lovely dream
That glitters through the snowy showers.

I am afraid to call you by
Your name.   A name — what need for saying ?
But let me feast my greedy eye
Upon your southern beauty straying,

Upon your face forgotten quite,
That calls to memory unavailing
Days fleeting, days of joy unfailing
Slain by a snowstorm in the night.

(C. M. BOWRA)

Yes, I have loved.   And the mad glowing
Of love's drunk pain is at an end,
The triumph and the overthrowing,
The name of " foe ", the word of " friend ".

There have been many. . . . Are all fleeting ?
Mere memories and shades of dreams. . . .
Strangely I call them up, repeating
The golden music of their names.

There have been many.   But a single
Charm bound them all in unity,
One frenzied Beauty made them mingle ;
Its name is Love and Life to me !

Passion mysteriously breaking,
Lifted above the world on high
I saw another woman seeking
The fated place where passions lie.

And those same words, those same embraces,
On greedy lips the tedious lure,
Shoulders with ever-fading graces. . . .
No !   Life unloving, empty, pure !

In my breast exultation surges ;
From mountain-summits deep in snow
I send an avalanche by gorges
Where once I loved and kissed below !

(C. M. Bowra)

The Steps of the Commander

On the door a thick and heavy curtain,
  Through the window night mists peer.
What is left of all your hateful freedom,
  Juan, now that you know fear ?

Cold and lonely is the sumptuous bedroom,
   Servants sleep in night profound.
Out of happy lands unknown and distant
   You can hear the cock-crow sound.

What can that blest sound mean to a traitor?
   Numbered now life's moments seem.
Donna Anna sleeps, hands crossed on bosom,
   Donna Anna dreams a dream.

Whose the cruel features, hard and frozen,
   That the looking-glass displays?
Anna, is the grave so sweet to sleep in?
   Sweet to dream unearthly days?

Life is empty, bottomless, and senseless!
   Now advance to battle, ancient Doom!
In reply, enamoured and triumphant,
   Sounds a horn in snowy gloom.

Then flies swiftly, splashed by flames at night-time,
   Silent, black, the owl-eyed motor on.
To the house, in darkness, the Commander
   With unsounding heavy steps has gone.

Door is opened. From the frost enormous
   Hoarse clocks striking in the nightly sky,
Clocks are striking. . . . " You asked me to supper.
   Are you ready? Here am I."

To the cruel question comes no answer,
   Comes no answer. Voices fail.
Dread is the rich bedroom at the dawn-hour;
   Servants slumber, night is pale.

At the dawn-hour it is pale and chilly,
   At the dawn-hour night's thick veil.
" Queen of Light! where are you, Donna Anna?
   Anna! Anna!" Voices fail.

Only in the fearful mist of morning
   Hours resound with their last breath.
" Donna Anna rises at your death-hour,
   Anna rises at your hour of death."

(C. M. BOWRA)

ALL that is finished, finished, finished ;
The circle of our days is done.
And what illusion, and what power,
Recalls you, Past, when you have gone ?

Some morning clean and clear as crystal,
By Moscow's Kremlin shall I be,
When my own land recalls my spirit
To its primordial ecstasy ?

Or Easter-night beside the Neva,
In wind and ice and snowstorm, shall
Some beggar-woman with her crutches
Move my still body where I fall ?

Or in the countryside I love so,
When the grey autumn rustles round,
In rain and mist shall the young vultures
Devour my body on the ground ?

Or in an hour of starless anguish,
Inside some room's four walls, shall I
Give in to iron fate's compulsion
And lie down on white sheets to die ?

Or in new life, beyond all semblance,
Shall I forget my former dreams,
And shall my memory of these Doges
Be all that now Kalíta seems ?

But I believe — not past pursuing
Goes all I loved with such desire,
All of our beggared life's poor trembling,
Our unintelligible fire !

(C. M. BOWRA)

Demon

BEHIND me you must go, behind me,
My slave obedient and true;
The sparkling mountain-ridges find me
In flight unfaltering with you.

Above abysses I shall take you,
Bottomless pits of mystery;
And there, while futile terrors shake you,
Is inspiration's strength for me.

Amid the ether's flaming shower
I do not let you swoon, but show
My shadowy wings and sinewy power
To lift you and not let you go.

Upon the hills in white resplendence,
Upon the unstained meadow-ground,
In beautiful divine attendance
My fire shall strangely burn around.

Know you how frail is that delusion
By which mankind is tricked, how small
Is the poor pitiful confusion
That by wild passion's name we call?

When shadows gather in the even
And my enchantment seizes you,
You wish to fly aloft to heaven
Through fiery deserts of the blue.

I gather you in my embraces
And raise you up with me afar
To where a star is like earth's places
And earth's not different from a star.

Then stricken dumb with admiration,
New universes you can see,
Sights unbelievable, creation
Made by my playful fantasy.

In fear and strengthlessness you shiver;
I hear you whisper: "Let me go!"
You from my soft wings I deliver
And smile upon you, "Fly below!"

Beneath my smile divinely winning,
In an annihilating flight,
Like a cold stone, you flutter, spinning
Into the glittering void of night.

(C. M. BOWRA)

Artist

IN summer-heat or in wintertime glistening,
Days when you marry, or triumph, or die,
I would dispel deathly boredom by listening
For a soft peal yet unheard in the sky.

There it approaches, and coldly I wait for it,
Wait to get hold of it, leave it for dead.
While my attention is strained ahead straight for it,
It pulls a nearly invisible thread.

Wind from the sea? or are singing-birds calling there
From Paradise? Does Time stop and stay fast?
Or is the May's apple-blossom a-falling there
In snowy rain? Does an angel fly past?

Time is prolonged. Every wonder it cherishes;
Light, tumult, motion around me appear.
Wildly the future reflects all that perishes,
Nothing is present or pitiful here.

Finally, force inconceivable filling it,
Strains a new soul from its birth to the day, —
Curses, as thunder, attack the soul, killing it
Reason, creative, subdues it, — to slay.

Then in a shivering cage I shut wearily
That happy bird who once flew about merrily.

This was the bird that would take death from me,
This was the bird that would set the soul free.

There is the cage. Heavy, iron I fashioned it.
Golden it gleams in the sun's setting fire.
There is the bird for you. Once so impassioned it
Swings on the hoop as it sings to the wire.

Clipped are its wings ; all by heart now it sings to me —
Say, would you listen and stand by the door ?
Singing may please you, — but weariness clings to me.
Once more I wait, and know boredom once more.

(C. M. BOWRA)

Voice from the Chorus

WE weep, how often, I and you,
Over our lives' poor pitiful ways, —
But if, my friends, we only knew
The cold and gloom of coming days !

To-day your darling's hand you press,
You played with her and smiled ;
You weep to find untruthfulness,
Or in your hands a knife caress,
    Poor child, poor child !

There is no end to craft or lies ;
No sign of death appears.
A blacker light will blind the eyes,
And madder planets sweep the skies
    For years, for years !

The last age shall be worst of all,
    And you and I shall see
The sky wrapped in a guilty pall ;
Laughter on lips shall freeze and fall, —
    Anguish of Not-to-be. . . .

You wait for spring, my child, but none
Will greet your eyes.
To heaven you call out for the sun, —
No sun will rise.
You cry, but crying, like a stone,
Falls down and dies.

Be happy with your lives and ways, —
Stiller than water, low as grass.
Oh if we knew what comes to pass,
The cold and gloom of coming days !

(C. M. BOWRA)

You say I am frozen, and dry, and apart, —
Yes, so long as with you I shall wait.
It was not for kind words that I hammered my heart,
Not for friendship I struggled with fate.

You yourself were more sombre, more brave, in time back ;
In the stars you could read well and mark
That the nights yet to come are black, endlessly black,
That unknown is the edge of the dark.

See, now it has come.   All the world runs astray,
And no beacon's alight anywhere ;
And he who knew not what the stars had to say
The encompassing night cannot bear.

And for them who knew naught of the days that depart,
Or how full is the oncoming night,
Exhaustion and vengeance have darkened their heart,
And in horror their lips are shut tight.

We had days big with hope and with confidence then ;
I was simple and trusting as you ;
With a child's open face I went forth among men,
Unafraid of what slander could do.

Tho' you search, of those hopes you will find not a trace ;
To far stars all has vanished to-day ;

And from those whom I sought with a glad open face,
I turn now in loathing away.

And the very same soul that then waited and burned,
That was ready to yield itself whole, —
By hate and by love it has been overturned;
It is burnt up and shrivelled, that soul.

What remains is the face with set smile and knit brows,
The shut lips and the sorrowful might,
That the blood of insatiate women arouse
And give fire to a beast's appetite.

Spend yourself not in sighs that will nothing amend,
And beat not, in vain, the shut door;
You will learn nothing there where the poor beasts are penned,
Among those that we called men before.

You must cover your face in a hard iron mask
And worship at sanctified graves;
With that iron to guard Paradise is your task
For a while from the maniac slaves.

(C. M. Bowra)

Russia, my life! are we tied to one fate for us?
Tsar! yes, Siberia! Ermak! and jail!
Does no repentance, no parting await for us?
To my free soul can your darkness avail?

What do you know? Faith in God were you treasuring?
What do you wait for your singing to say?
Chud has done follies, and Merya, measuring
Marches and roads ev'ry mile of the way.

Boats, yes, and towns upon rivers they hew for you.
— Where are the shrines of the Emperor's Town?
Hawks and wild swans on the steppes rose and flew for you. . . .
Out of the steppes a black mist settles down.

Over the White Sea and over the Black again,
Black when the nights are and white are the days,
Wildly, dumb faces' reflections come back again,
Eyes of the Tartars with flames are ablaze.

Gentle and lasting the sky's red is gleaming then
Night upon night over armies below. . . .
Why do you charm me so, mirage of dreaming, then?
Why do you play with my free spirit so?

(C. M. BOWRA)

THOSE who were born in years of quiet
Recall not where their ways are set;
Children of Russia's time of riot,
We are unable to forget.

From years that burn us ashes settle. . . .
Are you all mad? does hope send news?
From days of freedom, days of battle
The gleam of blood on faces shews.

All speechless. Those reports affrighted
Have made lips close together press.
In hearts that were before delighted
There is a fated emptiness.

Above our beds of death let curving
Birds wheel about in clamorous horde, —
Let others, more of Thee deserving,
Now look upon Thy Kingdom, Lord!

(C. M. BOWRA)

Vulture

O'ER sleepy fields a vulture broods,
In circle upon circle sweeping,
Watching the meadow solitudes.
A mother in her hut is weeping:
" Take bread, my son, take breast, and grow;
Obey, take up thy cross, and go."

Centuries pass. Loud blares the war,
Rebellion rising, hamlets burning, —
But thou, my country, as before,
Thy age-old beauty red with mourning !
For how long must the mother weep ?
For how long must the vulture sweep ?

(C. M. BOWRA)

WILD wind batters
Window-panes,
And hinged shutters
Rudely strains.

Hour of Mass on Easter morn,
Bells far distant, bells forlorn,
Deafness, darkness everywhere ;
Only guest, a wind in scorn
Batters on the barrier.

Through the window — void and black ;
In the darkness footsteps crack.
There the ice-bound flood breaks free,
There a Bride awaits for me.

How to vile sleep not surrender ?
How drive off that guest from here ?
Not give up my love so tender
To the cursèd stranger's care ?

How not throw the world away ?
Not despair of everything,
If my only guest's a wind,
Nothing but a wild black wind
On my household battering ?

Why, wind, batter
Window-pane ?
And hinged shutter
Rudely strain ?

(C. M. BOWRA)

VLADISLAV KHODASEVICH
(1886–   )

Temptation

" ENOUGH ! for beauty is not needed.
The sordid world's not worth a song.
Grow dim, O Tasso's lamp ! Unheeded
Lie, Homer, friend for centuries long !

" And revolution is not needed ;
Its armies dissipate and fade.
It has one crown for which it pleaded,
It has one liberty — to trade.

" In vain on public squares stands preaching
Harmony's hungry son to men ;
Unwelcome is his gospel-teaching
To the successful citizen.

" Content, and recking proudly of it,
On heaps where blossoming banners stand,
The scabs of drudgery and profit
He scratches with an itching hand.

" — Be off ! Don't trouble me. I'm selling.
— No bourgeois, and no farmer, I.
— I hide my profits daily swelling
— In flaming cap of liberty.

" Soul, here confined and sickly grieving,
On heaps of this dishonoured lot,
Look up to heaven for relieving,
But near, upon the earth, look not ! "

So speaks the wicked Heart in trying
To tempt the Soul's unsullied dreams.
" O earthly one," says Soul, replying :
" What knowest thou where heaven gleams ? "

(C. M. BOWRA)

12

NIKOLAI GUMILEV
(1886–1921)

The Captains

ALL knights of the green cathedral, in armour,
Who follow the compass on darkening seas,
Gonzalo, and Cook, La Perouse, and Da Gama,
Columbus, the dreamer and king, Genoese !

Carthaginian Hanno, the Gambia's master,
The mariner Sinbad, Ulysses the strong,
To the Cape the grey rollers are hurrying faster
As they sing of your fame in a dithyramb-song !

And you sailors of fortune, you great mastiffs royal,
Who keep watch upon gold in a port that you hide,
Arabian wanderers, truth-seekers loyal,
Who upon the first raft were the first men to ride !

And everyone minding, desiring, and looking,
Who has lost all his care for his fathers' lands,
Whose laughter is bold and whose whistle is mocking,
Who the grey sages' testament understands !

How strange, and how sweet, in your fancies plumbing,
With a whisper your intimate names to tell,
And again to divine the enchanted numbing
That was born for you once in the deep sea's swell.

Still, it seems, in the world, as of old, are places
Where the wandering steps of the crowd never go,
Where monsters still dwell in the woods' sunny spaces
And the pearls are agleam in the bright depths below.

From the trees the sweet odorous resins are flowing,
And " Look ! " patterned leaves are a-whispering,
" Here are bees that with gold and with purple are glowing,
Here are roses more fine than the red of a king ! "

Dwarfs scuffle with birds in the high airy stations,
And soft are the glances that girls' looks send . . .
As if were uncounted the constellations,
And the world were as yet not revealed to its end.

(C. M. Bowra)

Loneliness

I SLUMBERED, and the white waves washed me thus
Sailing my own boat on the sea ;
And, pale as death, in breakers mountainous
My country was revealed to me.

It's full of horses wildly galloping
And golden caverns of delight ;
But in it savage panthers wandering
Have eyes that flash with flames at night.

The patterned grasses marvellously gleam,
The rivers are as mirrors clear ;
But in the forests hidden mandrakes teem
And plants of evil and of fear.

On blue-white marble there I set upright
A lofty beacon-flame to shine
That those who sped along the waters might
In the far distance see my sign.

I promised them the plumes of ostriches,
But no one answered to my call
To turn and keep his boat from voyages
Where the disastrous waters fall.

An oracle all did in honour keep,
And judgment passed in days gone by,
That his heart must for everlasting weep
Who in his wandering comes nigh.

In slumber shadows drawing near I see,
And countries of the spring and noon,
But sad clouds weigh upon me heavily
In moonbeams of an opal moon.

My loneliness upraises every hour
A fiery scourge, to let me know
That I am doomed to conquest by the power
Of oracles told long ago.

(C. M. BOWRA)

I and You

YES, I come from another country,
   To your world I can never belong.
Tinkling guitars cannot please me,
   I want a wild desolate song.

I do not read my verses in drawing-rooms
   To black-coats and dresses like shrouds.
I read my verses to dragons,
   To the waterfalls and to the clouds.

I love like an Arab in the desert
   Who flings himself on water and drinks,
Not like a knight in a picture
   Who looks at the stars and thinks.

I shall not die in a bedroom
   With a priest and a lawyer beside me.
I shall perish in a terrible ravine
   With a mass of wild ivy to hide me.

I shall not go to a Protestant heaven,
   Open to all in tidy blue skies,
But to a place where thief and publican
   And harlot will cry : " Friend, arise ! "

(V. DE S. PINTO)

ANNA AKHMATOVA
(1889–   )

THE lime-trees by the open door
Breathe sweet and rich.
Forgotten on the table
A glove and riding switch.

A yellow disk of lamplight,
A rustling near at hand.
(But why did you leave me?
I do not understand.)

How beautiful the world is
In the morning cool and clear!
Be patient now, be good, my heart,
The dawn will soon be here.

And oh! you must be weary,
So low you beat, and slow.
The soul is immortal —
Someone told me so.

                  (R. M. HEWITT)

I SAID to the cuckoo: "Till I die
    Tell me how many years must pass!"
Pines were waving in the sky,
    Yellow light fell on the grass.
Came no answer: all was still
    In that leafy place.
As I walked home the wind blew chill
    On my burning face.

                (V. DE S. PINTO)

No, no, I did not love you, — gladly
Scorched though I was by such a flame;
And yet explain the strength that sadly
Still lingers for me in your name.

In front of me I saw you kneeling,
Like one who waited for a crown ;
And round your youthful head was wheeling
Death's silent shade to strike you down.

You went, — but not to triumph going ;
You went to death. Oh empty night !
My Angel, may you stay not knowing,
Not seeing my despairing plight.

But if white suns from Paradises
Shine on the pathway in the spring,
But if the meadow bird arises
Among the spiked sheaves, on the wing,

Oh this is you, I know it, trying
To converse with me from the grave ;
I see the shot-scarred hillock lying
Above the Dniester's bloody wave.

Days of renown and love forgetting,
Forgetting days of youth gone by,
And crafty ways, and soul's dark fretting,
Yet still your face, your fame unsetting
I shall remember till I die.

(C. M. Bowra)

ALL is sold, all betrayed, all is looted ;
Death's black wing has flashed past in its flight.
All is gnawed by a hungering sorrow, —
Why shines there for us such a light ?

By day the town breathes scent of cherries
From an orchard that none can espy ;
By night glitter new constellations
In the depths of the clear summer sky.

To the houses all fallen and filthy
The wonder is coming so near, —
And nobody, nobody knew it,
Though all longed for it many a year.

(C. M. Bowra)

You are far off, stranger mine,
Yet to you I raise my cry ;
In the clouds the candles shine,
Escort through the crimson sky.

O my stranger, quickly stare
To the right with shining gaze ;
For a crafty dragon here
Is my master many days.

And the dragon in his den
Shows no ruth or law to men,
And his whip hangs on the wall
That I may not sing at all.

That winged dragon tortures me,
Teaches me humility,
To forget my laugh's proud zest,
To be better than the rest.

O sweet stranger, hear oh hear
In a distant place my cry,
So that you may learn to share
In my grief before I die.

(C. M. Bowra)

OSIP MANDELSTAM
(1892–   )

Tristia

1

I'VE studied all the lore of separation
From grievances bare-headed in the night.
The oxen chew, and lingers expectation,
And in the last hour townsmen know delight ;
I keep the rite of nights when cocks were crying,
When, shouldered all a traveller's load of wrongs,
Eyes, red with tears, were in the distance spying,
And women's weeping joined the Muse's songs.

2

Who knows good-bye when words are being spoken,
What kind of parting waits for us, what is
The promise that the cock's loud cries betoken,
When the fire burns on the Acropolis ?
In some new life, when dusky skies are flaming,
When idly chew the oxen in the shade,
Why does the cockerel, new life proclaiming,
Flap on the city's rampart, with wings splayed ?

3

I love the ordinary threads, the steady
Weaving of shuttles and the spindle's hum.
Oh look and see flying to us already,
Like the swan's down, barefooted Delia come !
Oh the monotonous warp and woof of living,
How beggarly the tongue of pleasure is !
All was before, all will return reviving,
And recognition be our one brief bliss.

4

So let it come to pass : clean platters laden
With a transparent figure on the clay, —
Just like a skin that's bleached and cracked, a maiden
Will lean and look into the waxen play.

Not ours to ask of Erebus divination :
Wax is for women what brass is for men.
Only in war our fate has consummation,
And divination too will perish then.

(C. M. BOWRA)

BORIS PASTERNAK
(1890–   )

In the breeze, on a bough that is asking
If it's time for the birds to sing,
Like a sparrow soaked with the showers,
My lilac blossom, you swing.

The raindrop's a heavy button,
And the garden in spate appears,
Bespattered and wet and sprinkled
As with millions of blue tears.

My sorrow fostered and nursed it,
In the time of the thorns, for you ;
On this very night reviving,
It murmured, and its scent blew.

All night you tapped at the window,
Made the shutters shake in distress ;
Suddenly the sharp perfume
Ran forward along your dress.

Awakened by scented marvels
From those times and memories,
To-day the garden is gazing
With eyes like anemones.

(C. M. Bowra)

SERGEI ESENIN
(1895–1925)

The Herd of Horses

ON the green hills a herd of horses strays ;
Their nostrils blow the gold dust from the days.

From the high hills to the blue water's reach
They shake and drop their manes as black as pitch.

Over the quiet water their heads strain ;
The moon has caught them in a silver rein.

Snorting in fear of their own shadows, they
Must wait to toss their manes, wait till the day.

. . . . . .

About the horses' ears the spring day rings
With the first flies' delightful welcomings.

But when the evening on the fields appears,
The horses kick about and twitch their ears.

Their ringing hooves sound fainter as they pass,
Now fade in air, now hover in the grass.

Only the water stretches to the star ;
Sorrows along its surface twinkle far.

. . . . .

The sun has set.   Quiet is everywhere.
Upon his horn a herdsman plays an air.

With lowered heads, the herd stands listening
To what the shaggy herdsman has to sing.

And playful Echo into their lips glides
And takes their thoughts to magic countrysides.

121

I love your days, I love your nights' dark shade,
My country, and for you this song I made.

(C. M. BOWRA)

WHERE, my childhood's home, art thou,
Warm beneath the hillock's brow ?
And my little blue, blue bud,
And the sand where no one trod ?
Where, my childhood's home, art thou ?

Past the river sings the cock.
There the shepherd grazed his flock
And amid the water's play
Shone three stars from far away.
Past the river sings the cock.

Time, a windmill with a wing,
Makes the pendulum moon to swing
Past the village, on the grain,
Speeds for hours the unseen rain,
Time, a windmill with a wing.

Rain with arrows in a crowd
Has convulsed my home with cloud,
Mowed the blue bud from the land,
Trampled down the golden sand,
Rain with arrows in a crowd.

(C. M. BOWRA)

O FIELDS of corn, O fields of corn,
   An orphan's grief is mine ;
Heavy on my heart lies yesterday,
   But in my heart you shine.

The fleeting miles whistle like birds
   About my horse's mane,
And the sun is sprinkling lavishly
   Her holy healing rain.

O land of floods and agony
   And gentle spring-tide powers,
Under the masters Dawn and Stars
   I passed my schooling hours.

While in the Bible of the winds
   I pondered o'er the words,
Isaiah came and walked with me
   To keep my golden herds.
           (R. M. Hewitt)

VASILI KAZIN
(1898–   )

The Bricklayer

I SAUNTER home in the evening,
And the sweat on my tired arms sticks,
But my apron into the darkness
Sings a red song of the bricks.

It sings how upward and upward
I climbed with my red load high ;
I was seen up there on the roof-top,
On the dark blue roof of the sky.

Like a roundabout whirled my eyesight ;
The mist in the wind made moan.
But the Morning too had a burden
And carried red bricks of its own.

I saunter home in the evening,
And the sweat on my tired arms sticks,
But my apron into the darkness
Sings a red song of the bricks.

(C. M. BOWRA)

VLADIMIR MAYAKOVSKY
(1893–1930)

Our March

TRAMP squares with rebellious treading !
Up heads ! As proud peaks be seen !
In the second flood we are spreading
Every city on earth will be clean.

Pied days plod.
Slowly the years' waggons come.
Speed's our god.
Hearts are beating a drum.

What gold is than ours diviner ?
Can the waspy bullets sting ?
Than our songs no weapons are finer.
Our gold is in shouts that ring.

Green let the grass grow,
Covering days past.
Rainbow, gleam, glow.
Let galloping years travel fast.

Do not look to the stars or bother ;
Without them our singing shall blow.
Oh, ask, Great Bear, our mother,
That alive to the stars we go !

Drink of delight ! Drink ! Shout !
Veins with the spring-flood thrumming.
Hearts up ! Strike out !
Our breasts are brass cymbals drumming.

(C. M. BOWRA)

NOTES

p. 2. *Girls' Song*, from *Evgeny Onegin*, canto III.

p. 7. *Tatyana's Letter*, from *Evgeny Onegin*, canto III.

p. 10. *May 26, 1828*, written on Pushkin's twenty-ninth birthday.

p. 10. *Remembrances*, one of the only three poems included by L. Tolstoy in his *Reading Book*. The other two are Baratynsky's *Death* and Tyutchev's *Silentium*.

p. 12. *Day's rain is done*. The poem is not unfinished, but as Pushkin published it.

p. 45. *Cossack Cradle-Song*. The refrain *Bayushki-bayú* means literally " I tell the story " but is used simply as a lullaby.

p. 49. *Dream*. Lermontov was actually killed in the Caucasus when fighting a duel.

p. 58. *Troparion*, from the poem *John Damascene*, is an imitation of the ἰδιόμελα of St. John Damascene which is part of the Requiem of the Greek Orthodox Church.

p. 71. *The Hungry One* and the two following poems are from Nekrasov's long poem *Who can be Happy and Free in Russia?*

p. 95. *The Coming Huns* was consciously inspired by Ivanov's *Beauty's Nomads*.

p. 97. *I have forebodings of Thee*, addressed to " the Beautiful Lady ", the object of Blok's early mystical poetry.

p. 99. *Autumn Love*, written in 1907, after the defeat of the revolutionary movement of 1905–6.

p. 101. *The Steps of the Commander*, based on the story of Don Juan in Mozart's *Don Giovanni* and Pushkin's *The Stone Guest*.

p. 103. *All that is finished*, written in Venice. Kalíta (l. 24) was a Grand Duke of Moscow in the fifteenth century.

p. 108. *Russia, my life !* written in 1910.
    (l. 2) Ermak conquered Siberia in the sixteenth century.
    (l. 7) Chud and Merya are old Russian tribes.
    (l. 10) The Emperor's Town is Tsargrad, the Slavonic name of Constantinople, which Russia has failed to reach.

p. 109. *Those who were born in years of quiet*, written in 1914 before the war and dedicated to the poetess Zinaida Hippius, contrasts the generation of the first Revolution with others.

p. 109. *Vulture*, written in 1916.

p. 114. *I and You.* Gumilev was shot in 1921 for taking part in a counter-revolutionary plot.

p. 116. *All is sold* and *You are far off*, both written in 1921.

p. 118. *Tristia*, written in 1918. The title recalls Ovid's poems from exile. In stanza 4 the reference is to the Russian custom of foretelling the future from the shapes taken by melted wax.

INDEX OF AUTHORS

THE END

Printed in Great Britain by R. & R. CLARK, LIMITED, *Edinburgh.*